Interpreting the Lessons of the Church Year

Norman K. Gottwald
Laura Lagerquist-Gottwald

PENTECOST 3

PROCLAMATION 6 | SERIES B

FORTRESS PRESS | MINNEAPOLIS

PROCLAMATION 6
Interpreting the Lessons of the Church Year
Series B, Pentecost 3

Cover design: Ellen Maly
Text design: David Lott

The Library of Congress has cataloged the first four volumes of Series A as follows:

Proclamation 6, Series A: interpreting the lessons of the church
    year.
            p.   cm.
        Contents: [1] Advent/Christmas / J. Christiaan Beker — [2]
    Epiphany / Susan K. Hedahl — [3] Lent / Peter J. Gomes — [4] Holy
    Week / Robin Scroggs.
        ISBN 0-8006-4207-4 (v. 1 : alk. paper) — ISBN 0-8006-4208-2 (v.
    2 : alk. paper) — ISBN 0-8006-4209-0 (v. 3 : alk. paper) — ISBN 0-8006-4210-4
    (v. 4 : alk. paper).
        1. Bible—Homiletical use. 2. Bible—liturgical lessons,
    English.
    BS534.5P74   1995
    251—dc20   95-4622
                                                                        CIP
            Series B:
            Advent/Christmas / Arthur Dewey—ISBN 0-8006-4215-5
            Epiphany / Mark Allan Powell—ISBN 0-8006-4216-3
            Lent / James H. Harris, Jerome C. Ross, and Miles J. Jones—
                ISBN 0-8006-4217-1
            Holy Week / Philip H. Pfatteicher—ISBN 0-8006-4218-X
            Easter / Beverly Roberts Gaventa—ISBN 0-8006-4219-8
            Pentecost 1 / Ched Myers—ISBN 0-8006-4220-1
            Pentecost 2 / Richard L. Eslinger—ISBN 0-8006-4221-X
            Pentecost 3 / Laura Lagerquist-Gottwald and Norman K. Gottwald—
                ISBN 0-8006-4222-8

The paper used in this publication meets the minimum requirements of American National
Standard for Information Sciences—Permanence of Paper for Printed Library Materials,
ANSI Z329.48-1948.

Manufactured in the U. S. A.
                                                                      AF 1-4222

00   99   98   97   96   1   2   3   4   5   6   7   8   9   10

Contents

Introduction

The aids presented here for preaching on Pentecost 3 texts are organized differently than in most commentaries on the lessons of the church year. A word of explanation is, therefore, in order.

The usual organization is to treat together the assigned Old Testament lesson, the epistle lesson, and the Gospel lesson in a Sunday-by-Sunday sequence just as they are printed in the lectionary. This arrangement has the advantage of highlighting the relations among the three texts on any given Sunday. From our experience, however, approaching the texts in this manner tends to downplay the continuity of Old Testament, epistle, and Gospel texts from Sunday to Sunday. In particular, it makes it difficult to do justice to the different literary genres within each of the three pathways that the readings follow. As a consequence, the distinctive way in which each of the biblical genres puts forth themes and issues may be easily obscured. Sermons following this approach may lose touch with the connections among the sequence of texts of which any single pericope is but a part.

The arrangement we follow is to group our comments according to the literary genres found in the assigned texts, thereby producing three pathways through the readings that correspond largely, but not entirely, with the familiar Gospel, epistle, and Old Testament clusters of texts. The first pathway is that of the *narrative* literary genre, which includes most of the Gospel readings plus Old Testament narrative texts. The second pathway is that of the *letter* literary genre, which includes the epistle readings in their entirety. The third pathway consists of an assortment of *Torah, prophetic, wisdom, and apocalyptic* literary genres, largely from among the Old Testament readings, but including New Testament apocalyptic texts.

These three pathways present the texts in the order given in the lectionary whenever possible, but several deviations occur in order to maintain the coherence of the genre groupings. To facilitate locating the discussion of each assigned text, the table of contents identifies all readings by their assigned Sundays and provides a page index to our discussion of the readings. Within the body of the book, our discussion of each pericope is also identified by the Sunday for which it is assigned. At several points we have supplied cross-references to other pericopes germane to the text under discussion.

The aim of this experimental organization is to combat the sense of textual fragmentation and discontinuity that sometimes afflicts use of the lectionary. By reading continuously through each of the three pathways, the preacher will gain a sweeping overview of the readings and a sense of the continuity and peculiar idiom of each of the sequences of texts. A decision can then be made either to develop a series of sermons following one of the genres, or to select texts from two or more genres. By tracing all three pathways at the start, it is our hope that the eventual design of the sermons will profit from the larger context in which they are seen.

It has occurred to us that the device of musical counterpoint, brilliantly exhibited in composers such as Bach and Mozart, provides a helpful analogy to differentiate these systems of organization. Counterpoint is the musical technique of combining two or more melodic lines in such a way that they establish a harmonic relationship while retaining their linear individuality. The linear melodies and their harmonic conjunctions blend within the listener's ear in a happy concordance.

Something akin to counterpoint is at work in constructing a lectionary of biblical texts, allowing of course for the clear differences between musical and linguistic texts. The sequences of Gospel, epistle, and Old Testament texts are the verbal "melodic lines," whereas the Sunday-by-Sunday conjunction of any three texts within these lines suggests "harmonic relationships." The traditional organization of preaching aids emphasizes the harmonic relationships among the texts, while the organization we offer emphasizes the flow and linear individuality of each of the melodic lines.

Finally, we have recommended motion pictures that may be used in conjunction with each sermon in several possible ways: by stimulating sermon ideas, by illustrative reference within the body of the homily, or by showing the film as a focus for group discussion on themes and issues presented in the sermon. Some of the films are explicitly on religious subjects, but many present their resonances with biblical themes in entirely secular idiom. In recommending these movies, we do not propose that the films themselves or the characters in the films are necessarily moral or spiritual models. Our aim is to generate life-centered reflection and discussion on the associated biblical texts and themes. In showing these films to church audiences, they should of course be researched and screened in advance to determine their suitability for various age groups within the congregation.

We welcome your feedback on the utility of this novel way of organizing a Proclamation volume.

The Narrative Pathway

The narrative genre is an inviting one for sermonizing since it is marked by vivid, dramatic plots that lend themselves to interpretive retelling. The designated narratives include a large number of well-known biblical stories that challenge the preacher to overcome glib familiarity with fresh readings of old stories. The narrative pathway through the assigned texts in the New Testament follows readings from Mark 10–13 and a pericope from the Gospel of John. The Old Testament narratives are drawn from Genesis, Ruth, 1 Samuel, and 1 Kings.

MARK 10:2-16; GENESIS 2:18-24 (20th Sunday/Proper 22)

Mark 10:2-12. Two incidents are recounted in the Markan pericope. In the first, certain Pharisees ask Jesus for a ruling as to whether divorce is permissible. Jesus grants that the law allows a man to divorce his wife, but only as a concession, since the intent of God in creation is lifelong monogamy. In discussion with his disciples, he extends this counsel to a woman who might wish to divorce her husband and brands remarriage by the initiating partner as adultery. In the second incident, children brought to Jesus for a blessing are initially rebuffed by the disciples, but Jesus overrules them and welcomes the children into his arms.

It was of course well known that the law allowed for divorce (Deut. 24:1-4), so it is suspicious that the Pharisees ask Jesus such a self-evident question. In his reply to the Pharisees, Jesus does not categorically renounce the divorce provision, but sharply relativizes it by declaring it to be contrary to the ideal of lifelong marital union grounded in Gen. 2:24. "Hardness of heart" in the Bible refers generally to an obduracy of will in which people persist on a course of action they know to be wrong.

In this instance, Jesus gives priority to the monogamous mandate of creation over the leniency of the law. In posing their question, the Pharisees speak only of a man initiating divorce. In his clarification to the disciples, Jesus adds the complementary action of a woman divorcing her husband. The prevailing view is that divorce was a forbidden recourse for Jewish women, although some believe that it may have been allowed in certain Hellenistic Jewish circles. Most interpreters believe that this evenhanded reference to both genders is a Markan addition since it would have been a permitted practice in his Gentile milieu whereas it would have been alien to the Palestinian Judaism known to Jesus.

The aim of the Pharisees in asking Jesus about divorce is far from clear. They may have adamantly supported the right of divorce, and thus were "testing" whether rumors of Jesus' opposition to divorce were true. On the other hand, in their speaking of Moses "allowing" divorce, they may also have been expressing some uneasiness about its appropriateness as currently practiced. There is the further possibility, at least as Mark sees it, that they were trying to draw Jesus into political "hot water" by bringing up divorce, the precise issue that cost John the Baptist his life for condemning Herod Antipas's marriage to his brother Philip's wife (Mark 6:14-29).

The text says nothing about the Pharisees' response to Jesus' interpretation. They may have been left in as much uncertainty as the disciples who go on to press Jesus for clarification. Judging from Jesus' statement to the disciples, their unspecified query may have concerned what attitude to entertain toward divorces that have already occurred and would doubtless continue to occur. Jesus' explanation to his disciples acknowledges that divorces do and will occur, but that remarriage of the divorcing partners is a form of adultery. He does not comment on remarriage of the divorced partner.

From this text we do not have the full mind of Jesus on divorce. The conclusion he draws from Gen. 2:24 is that since God joins husband and wife into "one flesh," no one is entitled to separate them, including either of the partners themselves. Does he thereby forbid any and all legal enactments of divorce, irrespective of circumstances, or is he bravely—but ruefully—holding up a "counsel of perfection" that he knows is too exacting for "hardened hearts"? Is he warning against "the easy out" taken by those who are unwilling to put in the effort necessary to repair strained first marriages? Is he protective of women who were far more vulnerable than men to loss of economic and social status from divorce? Is he expressing peasant disdain toward a practice considered an idle luxury among upper class men, such as Herod Antipas? Though none is articulated in the text, all these motives are plausible.

In addition to the usual number of unhappy marriages due to childlessness and personality differences, the sectarian life of early Christians must have put additional strains on marriages. Mark's report of Jesus' "ruling" on divorce was perceived as unduly harsh, so that in Matthew's version Jesus allows for divorce in the case of adultery (Matt. 19:9). The reasoning is apparently this: since the commandment against adultery has already been breached by one partner, the aggrieved partner could initiate divorce as a formal recognition that the marriage had been spiritually and morally broken in the act of adultery. In another Matthean version of Jesus' teaching on divorce, the stigma of adultery is not only extended to the man who would marry a divorced women but inexplicably to the divorcee herself who by the very act of being divorced has been "made an adulteress" (Matt. 5:32).

Furthermore, Paul recognizes divorce as a legal option for both husband and wife, but strongly reiterates Jesus' opposition to divorce. Nevertheless, if a woman divorces she should remain single. Paul presumably intends the same counsel for the man who divorces but he does not say so explicitly (1 Cor. 7:10-11). Paul also counsels faithfulness to non-Christian partners, but if the unbelieving partner wishes a divorce it should not be contested (1 Cor. 7:15). These various elaborations and applications of the enigmatic divorce teaching in Mark show that early Christians agonized over what to do about marriages "on the rocks" and adopted various coping strategies that sought to avoid divorce while trying to limit the damage in those cases where it occurred in spite of all exhortation otherwise.

Christians today are of divided mind, both among one another and within themselves. From the perspective of the spiritual and physical unity of marriage, divorce is rather uniformly viewed as a failure that ought to be avoided insofar as possible. Some hue resolutely to a strict interpretation of Jesus' counsel. It is widely recognized, however, that in many cases the actual failure of the marriage began with the casualness or incompatibility with which marriage was entered. From the angle of social harmony, including the welfare of children, it is now widely conceded that in certain cases it is in the interests of partners and their children to dissolve extremely unhealthy marriages. It is now common for Christians to divorce without moral or religious stigma. No doubt cultural trends toward individualism, the emergence of psychology, and the increasing economic resourcefulness of women have contributed to the relaxing of religious barriers to divorce. But for many it is felt to be an exercise of discerning Christian love to call an end to marriages that no longer upbuild the people involved.

Nonetheless, the troubled state of marriage in our society is cause for deep concern. A sermon on this text might well focus on the implications of two people joining in the "one flesh" of marriage. What does this unity consist of? **Genesis 2**, which introduces the concept of marital union, does not "flesh out" the contours of a couple being "one flesh," and almost at once, we see that first couple divided and at odds, engaged in the blaming game. In the light of unhealthy codependence, or domination of one partner by the other, how are we to distinguish true unity from illusory or imposed unity? How are we to protect individuality and cultivate creative conflict within the mutuality of marriage? What are the resources within the church to highlight and encourage the attitudes and practices that make for this true unity? These are some of the issues that a sermon based on the Markan and Genesis narratives could address. A constructive focus on the ingredients of marriage seems a wiser course than trying to preach on whether or when divorce is allowable or desirable.

Movie: *Once Were Warriors* (1994).

Mark 10:13-16. In the incident of blessing the children, no reason is given for the disciples' stern rebuke of those who brought them to Jesus. It may have been an expression of their protectiveness of Jesus' time and energy, mixed with an adult disregard for the interests of children. It is usually assumed that parents have brought their offspring to Jesus, but the vagueness of the text ("people were bringing little children to him") allows of another possibility. These children may have been unwanted and abandoned offspring, who had to fend for themselves and who were "fair game" for unscrupulous operators to organize as beggars and petty thieves. They would thus be comparable to other disposable elements of society whom Jesus welcomed. If so, the impatience of the disciples might reflect a cultural disdain for such social riffraff.

In any case, Jesus indignantly replies by highlighting the childlike qualities that enable adults to receive the kingdom of God. The precise meaning of the simile "as a little child" has intrigued interpreters without leading to consensus. Possibly its best explanation is found in comparing Mark 9:33-37 where Jesus takes a child in his arms in response to an argument among the disciples as to which of them was "greatest." Jesus declares that the welcoming of one such child is a welcoming of himself and of God. Welcoming the child as a welcoming of Jesus seems tantamount to receiving the kingdom of God. Correspondingly, in Jesus' mind the childlike quality underscored seems to be unconcern with greatness.

In the Markan community, it is possible that this pericope was directed to a debate about how best to incorporate children into the body of believers. A sermon on "receiving" and "welcoming" children might properly focus on how adequately contemporary churches regard and provide for children, particularly unwanted and uncared-for children. Since children in the biblical world, and to some extent in ours, are "nonpersons," a further extension of the text might be to ask, Who are the nonpersons in our situation whom we, as disciples, discourage from taking part in our religious institutions? Are they the racially and culturally "others," the poor, the homeless, the immigrants, the gays and lesbians, the handicapped? This line of reflection would accord well with the possibility that the children presented to Jesus were orphans or abandoned children, and thus among the defenseless and expendable members of society.

Most frequently one hears sermons on the childlike qualities to be encouraged in adult Christians. A major challenge to sermons in this vein is to avoid idealization and sentimentality about the virtues of childhood. Biblical societies did not hold such naive views of children, and we know better ourselves. In their own terms, children can be peevish and throw tantrums, and they can even quarrel about "who is greatest" within their small world, since there is an ego-centeredness in children that accompanies their naive openness to others. Jesus' point is hardly to be construed as a praise of "childishness" in adults.

Movie: *Oliver! (1968).*

MARK 10:17-31 (21st Sunday/Proper 23)

This inquirer of Jesus, commonly referred to as "the rich young ruler," provides a vivid example of exegetical harmonization of parallel Gospel traditions. Whereas he is called "rich" in all three traditions, he is a "youth" only in Matthew (19:20) and a "ruler" (of a synagogue?) only in Luke (18:18). In Mark, youthfulness would be inconsistent with the man's claim that he has kept all the commandments "since my youth."

Unlike some of the interrogators of Jesus, it appears that this man is sincere in asking what he should do "to inherit eternal life" ("enter the kingdom," "be saved"). Meaning to be polite and to show his trust in Jesus, and possibly to earn a "pat on the back," the man addresses him as "Good Teacher." Jesus takes offense at this opener, perhaps viewing it as overly fawning, and retorts that "no one is good but God alone." This takes the reader by surprise in the light of other New Testament traditions that claim sinlessness for Jesus. However, whereas Jesus frequently claims authority, he never claims sinlessness. It is the Christian community, looking back, that interprets the overall course of Jesus' life as a sinless life (see Hebrews). In spite of the man's opening "goof," Jesus is not deterred from responding to his question, or from "loving him."

Jesus reminds him of the commandments from the Decalogue that have to do with interpersonal relationships in community. Oddly, however, in saying "you shall not defraud," Jesus inserts a prohibition not strictly found in the Decalogue. This may be shorthand for the commandment against covetousness or selfish desire for what belongs to others. It especially points to cheating people of their wages, land, or inheritance (Deut. 24:14; James 5:4), and may be thought of as "robber baron" or "white collar robbery," in contrast to outright breaking in and petty theft, as in "You shall not steal." This freedom of Jesus in citing the commandments is "corrected" by Matthew and Luke who pointedly omit the commandment against defrauding others. There is, however, reason to think that Jesus deliberately referred to fraud because of the wealth of the inquirer.

The man at once claims that he has kept all these commandments over the course of his life. Jesus does not contest the claim, but moves immediately to propose what the man needs to do if he wants "to go all the way" to eternal life. He must sell everything he has, give to the poor, and follow Jesus. Why this severe requirement? Is this the step that would prove his complete devotion to God? Is this the move that would show his true understanding of the Decalogue? Is Jesus here challenging the very legitimacy of his "great possessions"?

To ponder such questions requires us to examine how people got great wealth in Roman Palestine. In short, they either acquired or inherited it through the expropriation of the lands of the indebted peasantry, or by tax collecting or commercial speculation, precisely the defrauding that Jesus inserted into his recital of the commandments. Jesus may be saying: If you really desire eternal life above all else, you must do what you can do to restore the goods taken from others either by you personally or by those who passed on their wealth to you. You have been your "brother's taker"; now it is time to be your "brother's keeper." Understandably, the rich man goes away sadly once he confronts the dire consequences of fully seeking eternal life.

In conversation with the disciples, Jesus extends his counsel to the rich man to include all those who have wealth. It is terribly "hard" for one accustomed to wealth to meet the demand for restitution to those defrauded. Yet it is not totally impossible. Jesus may here be speaking of a few he has known who were up to the demand. Although unmentioned by Mark, Luke tells of a tax collector who, upon meeting Jesus, voluntarily gave half of his goods to the poor, and from the remainder resolved to pay back anyone he had defrauded fourfold (Luke 19:1-10). The attempt to soften Jesus' judgment on wealth by arguing that the "needle's eye" was actually a narrow gate awkward for animals to pass through ignores the shock of the disciples at Jesus' severe remarks. Rich folk were widely regarded for their presumed piety. For the disciples to hear otherwise from Jesus overturns the cultural ideology of pious wealth that they had imbibed.

Peter turns the discussion to the situation of the disciples by asking in effect, "Look, unlike the rich man, we have given up everything and followed you. What's in it for us?" Jesus assures them that eternal life is "in the picture" for them, but the bulk of his response is to remind them of immediate rewards. He assures them that they will have their material and social needs met in the company of his followers, the new family of God. They are already enjoying eternal life in the kingdom fellowship on earth. The absence of reference to gaining substitute "fathers" for the biological fathers they have left may intend to underscore the more egalitarian nature of the Jesus movement in contrast to patriarchal family authority. It is widely thought that the reference to "persecutions" is an addition of Mark.

This story of the rich man who turned away has caused consternation among Christians through the centuries. A small minority has taken it literally and divested themselves of wealth. The major exegetical tradition has been to treat it as an exceptional case, presupposing that wealth was somehow an obstacle to this man's faith in a peculiar way that need not be the case with those fortunate wealthy persons who do not love their money. Others believe that Jesus meant what he said about getting rid of wealth, but refuse to follow his counsel, either because they hope to use part of it for charitable purposes or because they simply lack the religious motivation or courage to do so.

Sermons on this text have often grossly moralized and spiritualized the matter of wealth, instead of facing the hard issues presented. A better course would be to remind ourselves of the price that society pays for a few to be wealthy and many to be poor, and at the same time to attend to how seriously biblical traditions take the challenge to do economic and social justice. Sermons, joined with adult education courses and local community analyses, can help churches understand the national and local economic landscape. Who is hurting and why? In spite of tremendous obstacles, Jesus' words assure us that it may still be "possible" to put our wealth to kingdom use.

In a day when so many are losing their grip on means of livelihood, the church is challenged to offer more prophetic and pastoral economic services to its members so that Jesus' vision of a family of God caring for one another's needs could be implemented through our churches. Such preaching, to be more than idle dreaming, needs to recognize how much we who are so-called middle class "buy into" the notion that wealth is basically a very good thing for all of us. We who have enough "to get by" have swallowed the ideology that the wealth of a few prospers all of us—along with the seductive hope that we too might one day be wealthy—while we gloss over the tremendous suffering of the poor. Churches that cannot face up to this harsh reality are not listening to the gospel of Jesus in Mark.

Movies: *El Norte* (1984); *Roger and Me* (1989).

MARK 10:35-45 (22nd Sunday/Proper 24)

The request of James and John for positions of highest honor "on the right and left hand" of Jesus, once his kingdom comes to power, is foreshadowed in the argument among the disciples as to who among them was "greatest" (Mark 9:33-34). In Matthew, the request is more deviously made by the mother of James and John (20:20). These astute disciples sought a preemptive declaration from Jesus that would clarify their status and abort claims by other disciples for preeminence.

Jesus responds by asking if they have the fortitude to undergo the sufferings ("drinking the cup" and "being baptized") that Jesus has just predicted for himself (see 10:32-34). Without waiting for James and John to

reply, he assures them that they will do so (probably an *ex post facto* reference to their eventual martyrdom; cf. Acts 12:2), even though it is glory
and power that presently fuel their ambition. Then Jesus delivers "the stop-
per" as he informs them that he has no authority to appoint anyone as his
preferred assistants. Such honor is only for those "for whom it has been
prepared," an indirect reference to God's decision about such matters.
Understandably, the other ten disciples are affronted and angered by this
bold bid for power initiated by James and John.

Jesus then gathers all the disciples and instructs them in the nondominat-
ing nature of his kingdom. He contrasts it decisively with Gentile rulers who
"lord it over" their subjects. "It is not so among you." Nothing could attest
more clearly to the Jewishness of Jesus in claiming the egalitarian dimensions of his heritage over against the Greco-Roman style of rulership that he
and his disciples knew so well. If James and John, or any followers of Jesus,
aspire to preeminent leadership, they must do so by practicing servanthood.
The stellar example of this servanthood is the mission of the Son of Man
(see Dan. 7:9-14) who comes to serve and give his life as a ransom that liberates many from the slavery of competitive striving for greatness. Whether
this last remark is from Jesus or Mark, it nonetheless construes the tenor of
Jesus' life as a life of self-giving and not of prerogative-claiming.

This teaching about the obligatory servanthood of leaders must have
been painfully relevant to the Markan community and to all subsequent
Christian communities in which the tradition was received. An abiding
issue in the early Christian community concerns the nature of leadership as
an honor bestowed on those who serve rather than exploit. The New Testament writings are replete with warnings against lax or abusive conduct by
church leaders who fail to serve and admonitions to maintain unity in preference to factional rivalry and the cult of personality.

A sermonic option on this text is to examine notions and practices of
leadership in the preacher's congregation, set in the context of prevailing
leadership styles in the denomination, the church at large, society, and politics. Temptations to seek personal honor and prestige without serving actual
needs are ever at hand in religious organizations, especially in a societal cli-
mate that overemphasizes individual attainment and superficial signs of
success. There is a particular vulnerability of ministers as authority figures
to exaggerated self-importance that is dangerous when combined with dam-
aged egos. Preaching on this text will have maximal effect if accompanied
by feedback from the congregation and self-study of the actual patterns of
service throughout the church organization. It is easy to deceive ourselves
about the scope and relevance of the church "services" we offer.

Movies: *Brother Sun, Sister Moon* (1973); *Hombre* (1967).

MARK 10:46-52 (23rd Sunday/Proper 25)
MARK 11:1-11 (Christ the King Sunday/Proper 29)

A blind beggar is in the roadside crowd as Jesus passes through Jericho enroute to Jerusalem. He hears that Jesus of Nazareth is passing by. Refusing to be silenced, his clamorous cries for help are heard by Jesus who—because of the man's faith—heals him of his blindness. Told he is free to go, he chooses to follow Jesus on the way.

This is the only instance in Mark where a person healed is identified by name ("Legion" is a typological name uttered by the demons, not the actual name of the demoniac in Mark 5:9). The name Bartimaeus may have adhered in the tradition because he was remembered as a convert in one of the early Christian communities. The story is striking in circumstantial detail and electric with the insistence of Bartimaeus to be heard above the noise of the crowd and his agility when, throwing off his cloak, he springs forth to answer the summons of Jesus.

As with the woman cured of her long-standing hemorrhage (Mark 5:24b-34), Jesus tells Bartimaeus that his faith has made him well. In both instances, the faith of the supplicants is foregrounded by their bold actions: the woman presses forward in the crowd and actually touches Jesus, the man shouts out to Jesus all the louder as he is told by others to shut up. Even the faith of those bringing the person for healing can be efficacious, as in the case of those who lowered the paralytic through the roof (Mark 2:4-5) and the father of the epileptic boy (Mark 9:23-24). Faith is demonstrated by taking socially disapproved action in order to secure healing.

Especially prominent in this story is the title Bartimaeus uses twice in addressing Jesus as "Son of David." No one else in Mark addresses Jesus as Son of David. Most often Jesus is addressed, both by disciples and inquirers, as "Teacher," and occasionally as "Rabbi," and Jesus refers to himself as "The Teacher" (Mark 14:14). The clue to Mark putting the title "Son of David" on the lips of Bartimaeus is probably to be found in the ensuing entry into Jerusalem where the crowd hails Jesus with the acclamation, "Blessed is the coming kingdom of our ancestor David!" (Mark 11:10). It is easy to envision Bartimaeus, having followed Jesus all the way from Jericho, among those hailing him on his entry into Jerusalem. Mark displays purposeful dexterity in deploying titles for Jesus. While incorporating the Son of David title in his Gospel in spite of reservations about it (Mark 12:35-37), Mark strongly prefers the titles "Messiah" (Christ) and "Son of God" (Mark 1:1; 14:61; 15:39). He also faithfully records apocalyptic Son of Man references in the teaching of Jesus, but Jesus is not addressed as Son of Man anywhere in the Gospel and Mark does not employ it for his own characterization of Jesus.

The homily that seems to leap from the text concerns the astonishing power of single-minded, risk-taking faith. Bartimaeus falls into company with the other faith-driven supplicants mentioned above, to whom we might well add the Syro-Phoenician woman (Mark 7:24-30). Although faith is not mentioned as such in her case, the woman's sharp retort to Jesus' acerbic dismissal of her as a Gentile, leads to her daughter's healing ("For saying that, you may go—the demon has left your daughter," v. 29). It may even be concluded that the Gentile woman taught the Jewish Jesus something about the inclusiveness of human faith and divine love. Such a sermon might focus on these questions: What healings do we want Jesus to bring to us as individuals, congregations, communities, and as a nation and a world? What investments of faith on our part are necessary to attain such healings? What steps in faith are within the grasp of those who will hear this sermon?

Movies: *The Miracle Worker* (1962); *The Elephant Man* (1980).

MARK 12:28-34; RUTH 1:1-18 (24th Sunday/Proper 26)

A sympathetic scribe asks Jesus what he understands to be the primary commandment of the law. Jesus replies with a recitation of the *Shema* (Hear, O Israel!) with its declaration of the command to love God with one's whole being (Deut. 6:4-5), to which he quickly adds the second command to love one's neighbor (Lev. 19:18). The scribe enthusiastically concurs, adding that observing these commands is of higher priority than making cultic sacrifices. Jesus closes the exchange by declaring the scribe near—or even within—the kingdom of God.

Considering the way Mark focuses on the generally critical and hostile approach of the religious leaders to Jesus, the cordial open-minded stance of this scribe is noteworthy. Both Matthew (22:34-35) and Luke (10:25) reject Mark's portrait of the scribe by changing him into an opponent trying to entrap Jesus. By contrast, Mark takes care to explain why one of the normally hostile scribes approaches Jesus in so positive a way. Having overheard the previous exchange between Jesus and Sadducees on the topic of the resurrection of the dead, and being impressed by Jesus' line of argument, the scribe is prompted to ask Jesus a question of his own. Jewish interpreters of the law frequently engaged in efforts to give an overarching order and rationale for the more than six hundred separate commandments. So, in effect, the scribe is asking Jesus what "spin" he puts on the laws, what he takes to be their primary thrust.

That Jesus links the commands to love God and neighbor is not exceptional; the connection is made in other Jewish writings. In fact, in the Lukan version, where the scribe is trying to entrap Jesus, it is the scribe himself who volunteers the two commandments, and his way of being contentious is to ask Jesus, "Exactly who is my neighbor?"(Luke 10:25-29). In Mark, the friendly scribe responds to Jesus profusely, "You are right . . . you have truly spoken." Mark then has the scribe repeat practically verbatim what Jesus has said, no doubt to underscore the scribe's total comprehension of the priority of the commands. Not content to stop with a summary of what Jesus has said, he goes on to remark that these love commands are "much more important" than ritual sacrifices (drawing on 1 Sam. 15:22 and Hosea 6:6). This downplay of ritual accords with the Markan understanding of the outmodedness of Jewish ritual as expressed in Jesus' teaching on ritual uncleanness (Mark 7:1-23) and in the forecast of the destruction of the Temple (Mark 13), which had probably already occurred at the time of the Gospel's composition.

The scribe's exuberant reception of Jesus' way of prioritizing the commandments so impresses Jesus that he returns the approbation the scribe accorded him. As the scribe perceived Jesus to have answered the Sadducees "well," so Jesus takes note that the scribe has answered him "wisely." Jesus then declares, "You are not far from the kingdom of God." In saying this, Jesus is not telling him that he has "almost made it" to the kingdom but must do other things in order to reach it. It is a figure of speech known as a *litotes*, in which an affirmative is expressed by the negation of its opposite. In effect Jesus says, "You are near the kingdom of God." The understatement in the figure of speech may even carry the connotation, "I have nothing more to say because you are well within the kingdom of God."

A sermon on the link between love of God and love of neighbor could well be "ecumenical." It could stress how those who are in "opposite camps" socially or religiously (such as the scribe and the lay Jesus) can come together around the affirmation of love of God and neighbor, how their very honoring of one another is in itself already an act of neighborliness in fulfillment of the command. They are able to do this even if they practice different religious rituals, or none at all. Or, to follow up the Lukan tack on the incident, which sets up the Parable of the Good Samaritan, we might ponder the strange initiatives and reciprocities of neighborliness. If the surly scribe in Luke wants to hair-split over which neighbor he should love, the "answer" he gets in the parable shifts the focus entirely to show the unanticipated spectacle of ordinarily hostile "others" (in this case a Samaritan!) treating *us* as neighbors. The pericope from Ruth gives an instance of a "foreign woman," a Moabite woman who goes beyond duty to stay with her Israelite mother-in-law and expose herself to life in a strange land by accompanying Naomi to live in Bethlehem. Sometimes the one who needs "neighbor love" is in our own family!

The wide scope of these commands to love releases us both to extend neighborliness toward and receive neighborliness from anyone we encounter. For our churches, the bridging of race, class, gender, and age are inviting arenas for fulfilling the commandments. How do we follow this command when increasingly we do not even know the people who live nearby us? Moreover, how are we to practice the command to love God and neighbor if our church and society are structured so that we do not meet many people unlike ourselves, and what we know about them is mostly unflattering or demeaning stereotypes? What if we have to go out of our way to love those of other races, cultures, and classes? Do our churches help us do that in their education and outreach programs? Can we identify neighbors among the low income and marginal folk who typically get short shrift when it comes to funding for public services? What is the public social responsibility of Christian neighborliness? Clearly, the deceptively simple-sounding commands give us no occasion for smugness. If we penetrate them as deeply as Jesus and the inquiring scribe did, a major shift in attitudes and prioritizing might enter our lives, leavening our often self-centered congregations and impacting our discourse about public policy.

Movies: *Babette's Feast* (1987); *Schindler's List* (1993).

MARK 12:38-44; I KINGS 17:8-16; RUTH 3:1-5; 4:13-17 (25th Sunday/Proper 27)

In the course of teaching in the temple precincts, Jesus cautions wariness toward the scribes who were the religious scholars of his day, responsible for interpreting the law, and who sought to live righteously in keeping with the law. What troubles Jesus is that they make a great display of their piety and expect to be honored and deferred to at the same time they are abusing widows by grabbing up their means of livelihood. Jesus then watches people putting money into the temple treasury, including some sizable gifts by the rich. He singles out a widow who puts in two small coins and notes that by giving all that she had to live on—at least for the moment—she has given more than those who contributed large gifts out of their abundance. Interpretation of this pericope has traditionally revolved around two points: the fairness of Jesus' criticism of the scribes and the presumed exemplary force of "the widow's mite."

As for the tenor and accuracy of Jesus' criticism of the scribes, we need to note several things. First, the warning about the scribes in Mark is terse and moderate compared to the more extensive diatribes in the parallel passages of Matthew and Luke. This suggests that Matthew and Luke have intensified and embroidered Jesus' criticisms because of heated controversies with Jewish synagogues in their own settings some decades later. The heat and passion of later Jewish–Christian rivalry is retrojected by Matthew and Luke into the attitude of the historical Jesus. Mark obviously knows of the separation between Jews and Christians in his day, and he notes disagreements between them over keeping aspects of the ritual laws which he believes to be superseded in Christian piety. But he is clearer and more consistent than the other Gospels in showing that the basic controversy swirling around Jesus in his lifetime had to do with disputes among Jews over the interpretation of the law that all held in high regard as a vital part of their heritage.

Mark also shows that the opposition to Jesus, and the plan to execute him, was lodged in the professional Jewish leadership. The severe criticisms Jesus levels at these religious leaders is in line with the prophetic criticisms of the Old Testament and are no more anti-Semitic than the strictures of Amos or Isaiah. Furthermore, typical anti-Semitic allegations that Jews are evil because they are Jews, and that Jews are more evil than non-Jews, are completely absent both from the lips and from the conduct of Jesus of Nazareth. Mark himself is probably a Hellenistic Jew, but he is emphatically not a "self-hating Jew." Neither to Jesus nor to Mark are the scribes reprehensible simply because they are Jews but some of them are reprehensible because they are abusive religious professionals who prey on fellow Jews.

There is of course the issue of how many scribes and priests behaved in this abusive way, and whether Jesus intended his remarks as a condemnation of all scribes. It is not likely that he did. It is important to recognize that scribes did not occupy a single socioeconomic niche; some were of quite ordinary status and means, while others were prestigious and rich. It is these latter highly placed scribes and priests who seem to be those most adamant in opposing Jesus and whom he in turn criticizes. From the preceding pericope we know that, from Jesus' perspective, some scribes were ethically honorable men who subordinated ritual to love of God and neighbor. Jesus was thus fully aware that scribes were not automatically sinful. Nevertheless, he saw too much abuse to be overlooked, and he viewed the entrenched power and privilege of certain scribes and priests as unjust and conducive to disregard and oppression of the socially vulnerable and expendable.

The criticisms Jesus makes of the scribes are twofold. First, as many of his controversies with them show, he held a more flexible view of the application of the law to human needs (2:1-12; 7:1-23). Second, as in this pericope, he objects to their combination of ostentatious piety and social oppression. He advises against the type of "showy" piety that exalted their own egos without sufficient regard for the real needs of people. Like the prophets before him, he is especially outraged at pious leaders who do wrong to the socially vulnerable.

Among the most vulnerable in biblical society were widows who lacked the support of grown sons or protection from relatives. The assigned Old

Testament readings illustrate the plight of two widows: the woman of Zarephath (1 Kings 17:6-16) and Naomi (Ruth 3:1-5; 4:13-17). The widow visited by Elijah during a great famine is about to eat her last meal. When she shares the meal with the prophet, she is blessed with an unfailing supply of food. Soon thereafter, her young son falls severely ill and she faces the prospect of being the sole family survivor, but Elijah further intervenes to restore her son to health (vv. 17-24). In a related incident, the widow of one of the prophets in Elisha's company is about to lose her two children to a creditor as debtor slaves. Elisha provides her with enough oil to pay off the debt and support her family (2 Kings 4:1-7). The other widow, Naomi, has lost her husband and both her sons, but has the support of her widowed daughter-in-law Ruth. Naomi is resourceful in arranging the marriage of Ruth to a wealthy kinsman who, in marrying Ruth, also "redeems" by purchase a small plot of land that had belonged to Naomi's husband (4:1-10).

It is evident that many widows were not so fortunate as to have a prophet or a wealthy kinsman to rescue them from their distress. Indeed, they were sometimes the victims of unscrupulous religious leaders who duplicitously befriended them. Jesus warns to watch out for scribes who take advantage of widows by "devouring" their property and thus depriving them and their offspring of livelihood. It appears that financially inexperienced widows, suddenly in charge of the disposition of property bequeathed to them by their deceased husbands, resorted to advice from scribes, and in some cases turned over the administration of their property to scribes as legal experts, only to discover later that they had been defrauded. Jesus may also have in mind the "sales pitch" of scribes who encourage widows to give their inheritance to the temple treasury, leaving them without adequate means of livelihood.

This brings us to the attitude of Jesus toward the act of the pious widow who puts her last pittance into the temple treasury. Customarily it is assumed that Jesus lauds the woman for her gift because she has given "all that she has." It is to be noted, however, that Jesus does not praise the woman's gift per se; he only observes that proportionate to her means it is a more substantial gift than those of the rich. This evaluation of Jesus, taken in context with the condemnation of scribal abuse of widows, suggests that he is underscoring the economic ruthlessness of scribes and priests in the particular instance of a widow who has been persuaded by religious ideology to divest herself of what little she has. The stress in the statement of Jesus is less on the generosity of the widow than on the abundance of the rich who include well-heeled scribes, part of whose wealth has come from defrauding widows at the same time they encourage those same widows to support the religious establishment with what meager means has been left to them. Jesus' comment about the respective gifts of the widow and the rich is best understood as an ironic lament. In the name of the same religion, scribes take all and widows give all.

While professional Christian leaders do not have the precise duties of ancient Jewish scribes, the parallels are close enough to generate sermonic reflection about abuse of leadership in the context of the duties and responsibilities of office. Do we clergy, and other professional church leaders, parade our piety and insist on preferred treatment? Do we cling to our prerogatives and shy away from delegating or sharing leadership? Do we do wrong to those in our charge by ignoring their full human needs as we focus narrowly on their duties to the church? Do we shape church priorities and policies to suit the big givers and pay less attention to the voices of those who have little to give? Most clergy do not have opportunity to enrich themselves on a scale open to the ancient scribes, but we do have status as leaders and we do often negotiate issues in the church with people who have money and social power.

Whose welfare are we serving in our conduct of office? Do we overtly or subtly ignore or devalue some people we are called to serve? Do we minister as readily to the little givers as to the big givers, and do we strive to counteract the social tendency to dismiss those who have modest means, or are in other ways discounted by society at large? In this category of "widow-like" folk, one thinks of divorced persons, the handicapped, the uneducated, the elderly, the racially or culturally "others," gays and lesbians, the homeless, and the unemployed. A sermon on this pericope might well ask, Which of these, or other discounted folk, pose a particular challenge to the inclusiveness of this congregation?

Movies: *Elmer Gantry* (1968); *Thy Kingdom Come . . . Thy Will Be Done* (1988).

I SAMUEL 1:4-20 (26th Sunday/Proper 28)

This narrative about the desperate longing of a childless woman to have a son is tenuously connected with the other readings for this day from Daniel 12 and Mark 13. They are conceivably related by the broad theme of "a time of anguish and deliverance for God's people." The narrative explains the circumstances leading to the birth of Samuel in a pious Israelite family. It exhibits the familiar Israelite motif of the devout barren wife who eventually conceives a son with the help of God (cf. Sarah and Samson's mother). It also introduces the motif of rival wives who are ranked by society and by themselves according to their success in childbirth (cf. Rachel and Leah). The story contains touching scenes of the close emotional relationship between Hannah and her husband and of her sadness and bitterness at being infertile. It also introduces Eli, the priest, whose line will be replaced by the yet-unborn Samuel.

Elkanah and his two wives Hannah and Peninnah, accompanied by the latter's sons and daughters, were in the habit of going on a yearly pilgrimage to the temple at Shiloh where they offered sacrifices. Elkanah is grieved at Hannah's barrenness and at the taunting she has to endure from his other wife, to the extent that he tries to console her by giving her an extra large share of meat from the animal sacrifice he has made. He assures her that she means more to him than any number of sons she might bear.

On the occasion recounted in the story, Hannah is so disconsolate that she refuses to eat or drink. She goes to the temple in her distress and silently beseeches God for a son, promising that, if her request is granted, she will dedicate the new-born to service as a Nazirite, a kind of Israelite monastic order with strict rules of conduct. Eli, priest at Shiloh, observes Hannah praying. Evidently it was customary to pray aloud, but Hannah is so overcome with grief that she cannot voice her prayer. Eli takes her to be drunk and rebukes her for her indecorous behavior in the temple. The impression of drunkenness may have been furthered by erratic movements or mannerisms induced by her unbearable sorrow. When Hannah explains the cause of her anxiety and vexation, Eli sends her away with a consolatory blessing.

Hannah's agonized prayer and valiant vow, together with Eli's blessing, ease her great pain. She goes to her quarters, eats and drinks, sleeps, and takes part next morning in the family religious observances. Some time after returning from the pilgrimage, Hannah conceives and bears a son. She names him Samuel, because "I have asked (*shaul*) him of the LORD." This wordplay does not work for the name Samuel, but it does for Saul (= *shaul*). Many interpreters believe that the story originally told of the birth of Saul, the other principal character in the first half of the book. The motive for shifting the story from Saul to Samuel would have been to discredit Saul while enhancing Samuel. Subsequently, one strand of tradition in 1 Samuel pictures Saul as a failed king because he has disobeyed divine instruction given through Samuel. Actually, neither Samuel nor Saul is later described as being a Nazirite.

The story lends itself to sermons about family life under disappointing constraints: in this case, the personal pain and social stigma of childlessness for wife and husband. Infertility is a growing concern for many couples who suffer in silence. The church has the opportunity to give voice to this form of suffering as Eli helped Hannah; more widely, to the strain of any devastating loss or disappointment on the whole family. Peninnah typifies the family member who sows division by turning on the person suffering loss. Elkanah typifies the family member who seeks to console and share the burden of pain and loss. Hannah typifies the family member in deepest distress who is nearly overwhelmed by her loss until she is able to commit matters to God, talk about her grief and hope with an empathic out-sider, and then "let go." Losses of goods, meaningful work, close relation-ships, social recognition, honor and reputation, and health can debilitate families. How well do our congregations admit to such dispiriting events and what resources do they offer to support people living through them? Eli's initial response was to look only at the surface symptoms of grief; he had to go deeper into Hannah's actual loss before he could aid her in any way. Would the attitudes and practices of this congregation make it a place where someone like Hannah could find understanding and support?

Movies: *Abraham* (1994); *Shadowlands* (1993).

JOHN 18:33-37 (Christ the King Sunday/Proper 29)

Jesus is brought to Pilate for interrogation to determine if he is guilty of death. There is a spirited verbal exchange between them, pivoting on Pilate's opening question, "Are you the King of the Jews?" Jesus counters with his own question, "Is this your question, or did others put you up to asking it?" Taken aback, Pilate disclaims knowledge of Jewish affairs, but still insists on an answer, "What have you done?" Jesus acknowledges his "kingship," but insists that its origin is not from the political power nexus of this world. He contrasts his "followers/servants," who are not fighting to prevent his arrest and trial, with the "temple police/servants" (same Greek word; cf. 18:3, 12, 18, 22; 19:6) who arrested and delivered him for trial. Seizing on Jesus' admission of kingship, but without hearing Jesus' qualifi-cation, Pilate presses for a direct answer, "So you are a king?" Knowing that he is unheard, Jesus retorts, "You say that I am a king," and goes on to describe his life mission in Johannine theological language: he came into the world to testify to the truth. Those who belong to the truth listen to his voice. The clear inference is that Pilate does not listen to Jesus because he does not belong to the truth. The pericope cuts off Pilate's closing question ("What is truth?"), spoken as it were into the air, neither expecting nor get-ting an answer from Jesus. It breathes not Pilate's profundity of thought but his opportunistic cynicism, as well as his frustration at the elusiveness of the "facts" in this capital case.

Pilate had not wished to get embroiled in the trial of Jesus, preferring to leave it to Jewish authorities. But they inform him that they regard it as a capital case which they are not allowed to handle. Opinions differ on whether the Sanhedrin could pass a death sentence under Roman rule, but even if they could have done so, it would strengthen their ties with the Romans if their judgment was confirmed and formally carried out by Rome (18:28-32; cf. 18:14).

Pilate in John's Gospel shows the harshness and political opportunism attributed to him by Jewish and Roman sources. Uninterested in ritual or theological niceties, he moves straight to the political issue: "Are you or are you not seditiously claiming kingship over Roman territory?" The answer he gets from Jesus seems contradictory: Jesus is a king who will not fight for his kingship! Struggling to resolve the contradiction, he tries again: "So you actually are a king?" But this gains him no further understanding because Jesus turns the question back upon him: "Well, you say I am a king, but the way I prefer to talk about my role is that of one who testifies to the truth." We could imagine this repartee going on *ad infinitum*, with Pilate trying to crack the conundrum of someone admitting he has a kingship/reign but who will not say he is a king.

That Pilate and Jesus talk past one another is partly explained by the theological perspective of the Johannine evangelist, evidenced in Jesus' closing explanation of his "kingship" as a testifying to the truth in a world where those who are untruthful cannot hear him. But even apart from the Johannine theology, Pilate is closed to the reality of a social and religious leader who asserts a moral and spiritual claim to lead the way into a new order of human relating that is not based on political and legal coercion. If this leader and his followers were to use military means, Pilate knows what to do about that. But if they do not challenge him overtly at his points of strength, Pilate cannot be sure whether the movement is merely harmless or devious, with a potential to cause trouble for Rome if it is not immediately squelched. Even if Jesus and his followers are innocent of sedition, the controversy they have aroused could incite other Jewish movements and factions and eventually erupt into civil disorder. Behind the clipped dialogue between the two men, the wheels of calculation are spinning in Pilate's mind. There is no point in executing Jesus if this is an internal Jewish religious quarrel that is no bother to Rome. But if the evasiveness and double-talk he seems to hear from Jesus mask genuine seditious intentions, or if Jesus may inadvertently trigger forces of disorder beyond his control, Pilate is prepared to execute him.

Translations have usually rendered Jesus' dictum as "My kingdom is *not of* this world," widely taken to mean that Jesus was a spiritual teacher offering individual salvation who had no interests and concerns in social and political matters. Ingrained as that notion is, it does not comport with the Jesus pictured in the Synoptic Gospels, nor—in spite of the dualistic thrust of Johannine theology—does it really do justice to the Jesus of the Fourth Gospel. The better translation, "My rule is *not derived from* this world," honors the source of Jesus' authority and mission in God but in no way excludes social and political matters as spheres in which his way of life is to be carried out. The teaching and conduct of Jesus touch and invade the social, economic, and political spheres of life again and again.

His notion of leadership in all areas of life as a service to human beings seen as equals before God and brothers and sisters to one another cuts at the root of social, economic, and political inequality and domination. Jesus of the Gospels stands as a continuing sign and testimony against all abusive structures in corporate life, including ecclesiastical structures. Jewish and Roman authorities, who were repeatedly inaccurate in the particulars of their suspicions and accusations concerning him, nonetheless correctly sensed that Jesus spelled trouble for their agendas of power and self-glory.

Sermons generated out of this pericope might explore the continuing power of Jesus to inspire and to judge the arrangements of our common life. Who is this Jesus, at once known and unknown, both invoked and ignored, by church and society? He seems an elusive and protean figure. He is readily cited by church leaders and surprisingly often referred to by leaders in civil society, especially when they claim to be following his example. He is just as regularly ignored by leaders within and without the church when he is felt to be naively irrelevant or when he touches raw spots in the priorities and procedures that shape our institutional life. It remains a comfortable "out" to consign Jesus to our private moralities and pieties in this life and to heaven in the next, leaving us to do the expedient things that have to be done to keep the world going on its familiar course. The worthy aim of such a sermon would be to establish the sovereign claim of God advanced by Jesus over all the realms of human life.

But there is a "blind spot" that imperils this grand vision. Jesus could make his claims within a homogeneous Jewish religious culture. His claims do not translate the same way into a world of various religions. We are not a homogeneous nation of Christians. We cannot construct a specifically Christian society, economy, or government. We are left to extrapolate from the historical Jesus a perspective and a set of criteria for the common good that we can argue and negotiate in the public arena with non-Christians. This is not as "compromising" as fundamentalist Christians often think. For in reality, neither Jesus nor the early Christians left us with the design for a Christian society, or a Christian economy, or a Christian government. We have to work from the particulars of the tradition about him, mediated through history, in order to discern the best possible arrangements of human life consistent with what we know about him. That is a mind-boggling task. But we can't even begin it as long as we think Jesus is concerned only with individual souls and private morality. What does it mean in practice that Jesus rules in absentia and that we are his servant-subjects throughout the entire fabric of our common life?

Movies: *The Brothers Karamazov* (1958); *The Mission* (1986).

The Letter Pathway

The Epistle to the Hebrews is a complex and puzzling writing, not much preached on except for the "roll call" of those who lived "by faith" (chap. 11). The lectionary readings from chaps. 1–7, 9–10 are samplings from an extended theological argument that the writer employs to encourage faithfulness among certain Christians whom he perceives as not only apathetic but on the verge of apostasy.

The focus in the theology of Hebrews is on the person of Christ as the culmination of the Jewish sacrificial cult. As the preexistent Son of God, Jesus on earth learns obedience through suffering, thereby qualifying as the superlative high priest who removes sin and returns to the heavenly realm (the temple above contrasted with the historical temple) to intercede for believers. The Christology in Hebrews is both "high," since Jesus comes from and returns on high, and "low," since—as earthly son of God—he achieves perfection in this life by obedience in the face of genuine temptation.

The practical application of this double-barreled Christology is to assure readers, on the one hand, that Jesus as high priest is uniquely willing and able to secure their salvation, and on the other hand, that Jesus as forerunner/pioneer is the perfect human example of faithfulness to God whom believers can and must emulate if they are "to hold fast" to their salvation. The author asserts emphatically, however, that those who fall away from their faith will not be saved, since Jesus provides all necessary heavenly and earthly resources to the believer.

Although dubbed an "epistle," Hebrews may not originally have been a letter. It has rather the form and style of a sermon, or perhaps a series of sermons revised and combined. It lacks the typical opening of a letter, although the conclusion is in letter form. The letter "sign off" may have been added when the author subsequently decided to send the sermon to one or more congregations, or it may have been added by another hand with the intention of imitating the letter form in order to establish the work's authority on a par with the letters of Paul.

Among those who regard Hebrews as a letter to a particular congregation, the most frequent theory is that it was sent to Christians at Rome. The proposed dates for the composition of Hebrews range from 60 to 95 C.E. The author is anonymous. The early identification of Pauline authorship does not stand (cf. the quite different content and style of Romans, Paul's most "theological" work). Clearly, the author was an awesomely gifted stylist, imbued with facility in Greco-Roman rhetoric and fluent in a type of figurative interpretation of Scripture influenced by late Platonic philosophy, and possibly by other conceptions of a sharp separation of heaven from earth such as those found in apocalyptic thought (as in the Qumran sect), Jewish mysticism linked to the divine throne vision of Ezekiel 1, or even pre-Christian Gnosticism. All these systems of thought made an emphatic distinction in kind between the human world and the transcendent world, although they differed in many other respects. Among early Christian leaders known from the New Testament, Apollos admirably fits the profile of the author of Hebrews (Acts 18:23-28).

In any case, whether preached or sent as a letter, Hebrews is addressed to the critical situation of certain Christian believers. The elaborate theological argument, replete with citations of the Greek Old Testament, speaks to a collective "you" composed of Christians who have survived hardship in the past but are now in danger of drifting away or renouncing their faith. They have known loss of property and imprisonment. One is inclined to think of the official Roman persecutions under Nero (54–68 C.E.) or Domitian (81–96 C.E.), but the persecutions alluded to in Hebrews may have been initiated locally on social and cultural grounds rather than as enforcement of the cult of emperor worship. Since the addressees of Hebrews have survived at least one severe trial of persecution, the author feels that their present unstable faith is the result of their misunderstanding or underestimation of the decisive salvation achieved for them by Jesus, and of their neglect of the examples of faithfulness provided by Old Testament figures culminating in Jesus himself.

It is the very skill of Hebrews with words and concepts that is likely to puzzle, even repel us, given our very different cultural and intellectual contexts. A major obstacle to understanding and appropriating the theology of Hebrews lies in its affinity to Platonic thought that was widely circulated in the first century in popular dress and had considerable influence on Hellenistic Jews, particularly Philo of Alexandria. The Platonic mode of thought held that the spiritual world of ideal forms was the true abiding reality, whereas earthly objects and persons were of value only as they reflected or approximated the ideal forms. The aim in much late Platonic thought was the cultivation of devotion to the ideal world by individuals who were thus released from the tyranny of earthly existence. Platonism, early and late, had an elitist stance that did not think highly of earthly life or of ordinary people who could not master philosophy.

The author of Hebrews employs two-world distinctions, influenced by Platonism, or similar thought systems, to contrast the earthly sacrificial cult of the Old Testament with the heavenly sacrifice of Jesus. Jesus is "superior to" Moses, Aaron, and even the angels, who at their very best did not attain the abiding realm of the heavenly, but only pointed toward it. Nonetheless, the issues over which Hebrews departs from Platonism are important and decisive junctures: first, Jesus was thoroughly of this earth and not a mere supernatural being who appeared on earth; and second, those who are striving toward the heavenly reality do so not as insular individual souls but as a corporate body, the Christian church, which includes all who believe—and not simply those with cultivated intellects, mystical leanings, or high aesthetic tastes.

The wedding of Platonic idealism and Jewish or Christian faith was highly problematic at best. On the surface, Platonism seemed to be compatible with the Old Testament cosmology of a heaven above and an earth below, but it lacked the historical concreteness of Jewish religion. In our day, traces of Platonism and other forms of philosophical idealism are encountered in the church mainly in a watered-down piety that spiritualizes religion by making it an otherworldly or inward matter involving God and individual believers. Apocalyptic two-world schemes, which may have also influenced Hebrews, affect the church by encouraging escapism and fatalism toward this world, even though such an escapist stance is diametrically opposed to Hebrews. Most Christians influenced by these reduced versions of Christianity probably have no knowledge of their Platonic roots and only a smattering of understanding about apocalyptic thought derived from popular "end of the world" books and TV programs. The philosophical and theological frames that make most sense in our world focus much more on historic existence here and now rather than on an ideal world above or yet to come.

It takes some effort to realize that the writer of Hebrews, while using a form of thought that appears to point individual souls away from the world, is actually modifying these two-world concepts in order to underscore the urgency of religious and ethical existence in the present for communities of faithful people. If this unique blend of Christian experience and philosophical world view in Hebrews is kept in mind, it becomes plausible to read it as a relevant homiletical resource in our day. Accordingly, the line of interpretation in the comments that follow will focus on the way Hebrew repeatedly marshals theology to achieve certain ethical and pastoral ends.

HEBREWS 1:1-4; 2:1-18 (20th Sunday/Proper 22)

Hebrews begins with a compact statement of the principal subject matter. The author locates Christian faith in firm continuity with Old Testament revelation: God, having spoken variously through the prophets, now speaks through his Son. This preexistent Son, of the very nature of God, has a cosmic status in creating and upholding the world (cf. John 1). This same Son, after accomplishing purification for sins on earth, now reigns in full power with God above, where his status is superior to that of angels.

This opener is interesting for what it says and what it does not say. It establishes that the Old Testament will be a basis for evaluating Christian existence, not by correcting the old but by fulfilling and exceeding its legitimate aspirations. It is intriguing that the earthly name of this Son, Jesus, is withheld until 2:9, where it resounds like a thunderclap ("But we do see Jesus!"). The slow build-up to identifying the Son as the historical Jesus intends to establish his cosmic authority in creation as the context for his earthly life. The Son's sovereign authority, derived from and presently exercised in the post-resurrection "ideal" world of God, securely anchors the achievements of the historical Jesus as Son of God. What Jesus did on earth is for the moment alluded to tersely, yet most significantly, by the phrase "made purification for sins."

Particularly striking is the claim that the Son is superior to angels. Angels are honored as "ministering spirits" of God (1:14) with "a valid message" (2:2). However, it is not to angels but only to the Son that "God subjected the world to come" (2:5). Reading Ps. 8:4-6 in a Christianizing mode, the author cites God's subjection of all creation to human beings who were "made a little [or "for a little while"] lower than angels." This exegesis becomes the springboard for presenting Jesus as the true human being in whom all things are subjected. The promise is that all things— especially sin and death—will be subjected to humanity, but we do not yet see that consummation. What we do see is Jesus who has gone through suffering and death and defeated sin for the benefit of all humanity. Jesus thus joins company with his redeemed fellow humans in achieving what is totally beyond the capability of angels.

This argument places Jesus firmly in the fellowship of the readers who are struggling with suffering, sin, and threat of death. The faithful journey of Jesus through earthly travail, in shared company with other humans, marks the process by which he becomes "a merciful and faithful high priest" (2:17). The prominence the author gives to angels alludes to the tradition that they were mediators of the law (2:2; cf. Gal. 3:19; Acts 7:53) and may also reflect belief in semidivine mediators within popular Platonism and related forms of Gnosticism, notions that found their way into Jewish and Christian groups (see Heb. 5:1-10). This is viewed by the author as a pernicious development, not so much because it is a "slap" at Jesus—as if the Son was jealous of his singular status—but because trust in angels mistakenly locates salvation in an otherworldly realm, whereas it has to be effected on earth in human action before it can be corroborated and certified in heaven. Jesus provided precisely the requisite earthly enactment of salvation that heaven ratifies.

A sermon on this cluster of ideas could be developed around what we Christians experience as the salvation brought by Christ. One need not get trapped in the niceties of the Old Testament exegesis or in literalizing the heaven/earth imagery. Amid the many attractions and benefits of faith in Jesus Christ, the author concentrates here on overcoming temptation, suffering, sin, and the power of death. What are the ways we experience temptation, suffering, sin, and death in our lives? How do we experience them as crippling bondage in our individual lives and in our life in church and society? How does Christ participate with us in those experiences and deliver us from them? His benefits to us certainly do not come from intellectual assent to a particular doctrine of the atonement, for there have been many theories about how Christ atones for and liberates us from sin. The salvation afforded us comes rather from an actual participation in the process of Jesus Christ's presence in our collective history and in our personal journey. What do we discover when we journey with others (or "run the race" of life as Heb. 12:1 puts it) in the company of Jesus?

Movies: *A River Runs through It* (1992); *Tender Mercies* (1983).

HEBREWS 3:1-6; 4:12-16
(21st and 22nd Sundays/Propers 23, 24)

This section of Hebrews calls the readers to consider the faithfulness of Jesus in his mission as apostle and high priest in order to strengthen their resolution to hold fast in their confession of faith. The fidelity of Jesus, in the face of grave temptation and suffering, forms the model for struggling Christians, since they can be assured that Jesus has known every form of temptation and suffering they undergo.

Having demonstrated the preeminence of Jesus over angels, the author now demonstrates the preeminence of Jesus over Moses, who was indeed a faithful servant in God's house (cf. Num. 12:7). A word play on "house" in several senses is introduced: "house" as the people of God in ancient Israel, as the whole created world, and as the body of Christian believers. Jesus, having been a "builder" in creation with God, is now more qualified than Moses to preside over the company of the faithful.

Between the two excerpts grouped in this lectionary reading, in 3:7—4:11 the writer plays on the pertinence for Christians of the Old Testament theme of "entering into rest" (quoted from Ps. 95:11). This repeated figure of speech refers to the endeavors of Israel to get through the wilderness and into the promised land, a goal that failed for an entire generation of Israelites because of their rebellion. The comparable "rest" for Christians is the realization of their salvation through Jesus that can only be attained if believers hold fast to their confession. Otherwise, they will meet the fate of Israelites who "hardened their hearts" (twice quoted from Ps. 95:8 in 3:7 and 15). The existential reality of the decision either to "harden" or "soften" one's heart is stressed by prolonging the "today" of the Psalm until it extends to the "today" of the Christian recipients of Hebrews. "While it is still 'today'" Christians can choose to hold fast to their belief and "enter the rest."

What is truly striking in the argument of Hebrews is that Christians are vulnerable to lapsing and losing their salvation.

Jesus may be a far superior mediator than angels or Moses, but Christians are just as susceptible to apostasy as were the Israelites of old. To be sure, they have a better resource of salvation and example of faith in Jesus than the Israelites had. However, for that resource and example to be effective, Christians must hold fast to their faith and renew it continually. Otherwise, to their shame, the wonderful work of Jesus on their behalf will be of no avail to them.

In 4:12-13 appears a vivid description of the swordlike word of God that cuts to the very heart of what people think and intend. This metaphor has often been simplistically attached to the Bible itself as the word of God. This is not the usage of the writer of Hebrews. To be sure, words of God appear faithfully in the Old Testament, and he wrestles with them to extract contemporary meanings. But the word of God is first and foremost the revelation of God in "the powerful word" of his Son (1:2), now freshly spoken in the earthly career of Jesus, whose fidelity penetrates Christian conscience as an inducement to faith—and as a latent judgment should the example of Jesus be rejected. Once more we see the incredible potency of Jesus to save, but only if he is received as the model of perseverance in faithfulness.

This extract from Hebrews offers opportunity to preach on the proper place of the Bible in the Christian life, as a witness to a living relationship with God but not as the object of magical faith. We see in Hebrews a writer with unabashed love of the Bible he was familiar with, which of course did not yet include the New Testament. He is saturated in the language and concepts of the Greek translation of the Old Testament, convinced of its traditions as the true witness to Christian faith. But not for a moment does he equate the Bible with God or with Jesus. They speak through the Bible, and what they say in the Bible is adjunct to what God and Jesus say to us in our lives. In this day of fundamentalist resurgence, including attempts to use words of the Bible as sloganeering prescriptions for political life, we need to revisit the Bible itself to be reminded of its servant role in attesting to the "living and active" word of God which keeps on speaking in every situation and moment in which we live. To paraphrase and extend the argument of Hebrews, Jesus is as much superior to the Bible as the living God is superior to all the "many and various ways" (1:1) in which deity has spoken to humanity, including the words of prophets and the acts of the cult recorded in the Old Testament.

Movies: *Black Robe* (1991); *Cry, the Beloved Country* (1995).

HEBREWS 5:1-10 (22nd and 23rd Sundays/Propers 24, 25)

After "demoting" angels and Moses to positions subordinate to Jesus, the author proceeds to do the same with the Aaronic priesthood. Jesus has been appointed high priest by God, as were all the high priests who preceded him. The decisive difference is that the Aaronic priests, being weak humans, had to offer sacrifices for their own sins as well as for the sins of others. In contrast, Jesus, by virtue of his obedient submission to God, has overcome all temptations to sin in his own life, and is thus competent to offer his very life as a sacrifice for the sins of others. The author typifies the priestly rank of Jesus in continuity with the priestly status of Melchizedek, a non-Hebrew priest-king who blessed Abraham (Gen. 14:17-24), and who is figuratively associated with the Israelite king in a royal coronation liturgy (Psalm 110).

This association of the priesthood of Jesus with the priesthood of Melchizedek is unparalleled in the New Testament, although Psalm 110, which cites Melchizedek as forerunner of Israelite kings, is cited in other New Testament writings because of its messianic association with David (e.g., Mark 12:35-37). Interestingly, there is a text among the Dead Sea Scrolls that presents an eschatological interpretation of Melchizedek. The text is a pastiche of Old Testament citations, very much in the manner of Hebrews, and it appears that Melchizedek is identified as the archangel Michael in another guise with royal and priestly characteristics (see Dan. 12:1). It becomes clear that Melchizedek was the subject of messianic speculation in Palestine as well as in Hellenistic settings. This increases the probability that the reference to Melchizedek as the type of a savior figure may already have been familiar to the first readers of Hebrews.

The exegetical thrust of Hebrews, not found in the Dead Sea text, is to extol Melchizedek as one who blessed Abraham long before the establishment of the Aaronic priesthood, and further to make much of the fact that Melchizedek has no genealogy (the Old Testament does not mention his father, mother, or descendants; 7:3). Hebrews takes this genealogical omission as the sign that Melchizedek is "a priest forever" and is thus the prototype of Christ (5:6; 7:3).

The exact force of the argument is difficult to determine. Does the author of Hebrews believe that Melchizedek still lives in the eternal Platonic world of ideal forms or in the apocalyptic heavenly realm? Or is this only a rhetorical flourish that should not be interpreted too literally? It is evident that, while glorifying Melchizedek, Hebrews does not conceive of him as a current rival of Jesus because Jesus has fully taken over the high qualities and functions of his Old Testament prototype. It may be that the prominence given to Melchizedek as the superior Old Testament priest who is in turn superseded by Jesus is aimed, at least in part, at discrediting the notion that Melchizedek is an archangel competitive with Jesus.

Noteworthy is the manner in which the author believes Jesus to be validated as true high priest in the order of Melchizedek. Jesus qualifies not through his glorious achievements as teacher or wonder worker, or even through his resurrection, but precisely through his submission to death. Jesus is described, in an utterly human way, as praying and imploring God "with loud cries and tears" (v. 7) to save him from death. At this point Hebrews may be reflecting the Synoptic tradition of Jesus in Gethsemane (Mark 14:32-43 and parallels). More astonishing still is the claim of Hebrews that Jesus "was heard because of his reverent submission." Hebrews evidently means to say that God heard and honored Jesus' prayer by not fulfilling his most urgent immediate desire to escape premature death. The goal of salvation for humanity thus hung on the slender thread of Jesus' resolve to be true to his calling in spite of his intense human inclination to avoid death. It is this extraordinary commitment to one's calling by God, even when it entails suffering and death, that sounds repeatedly in Hebrews as an inescapable challenge set before Christians who confess to follow Jesus.

What kind of sermon can emerge from this impassioned, yet oddly remote, kind of argument? Most Christians today are not given to fulfilling theological programs, since we seldom have strong leadings as to why and how we could serve God by "sacrificing" ourselves. The first recipients of Hebrews may not have been so different from us in their aversion to opposition and martyrdom. Yet, as a consequence of their identifying with Jesus as one who delivered them from sin and despair, they had come under social pressure and overt persecution. Life presented them a challenge, as it presents us challenges—challenges either to stand by or to surrender our deepest values and to "go with the crowd." Where are we challenged today to uphold or to desert the example of Jesus in pursuing our calling in company with him? Few of us are openly persecuted, but we are subtly pressured to forget the high standards of personal and communal integrity and self-giving exemplified in Jesus. We welcome him as the presumed "savior" from our sense of sin and guilt, but we are less disposed to follow him as "pioneer" and "forerunner" into a new way of relating to one another in community. Jesus feels companionable when we need comfort, but we less readily claim him as a model to undertake risky life ventures. Hebrews argues that we cannot have Jesus as savior unless we embrace him as our pioneer.

A sermon based on this pericope could ask: What are the challenges in our lives that we would prefer to avoid? What is asked of us that we would rather not risk? What are the benefits of "going beyond" our normal routine of self-guardedness? Do we, for example, shy from openness toward those near to us in family and work because distance and silence keep peace? Do we dismiss the world of social policy and political process because it takes time and seems fruitless to enter? In what ways do we "cut and trim" our commitments because they may be asking too much of us? What in fact are we committed to? Does our confession of Jesus Christ carry any recognizable responsibilities? If so, what are they?

Movies: *Long Day's Journey into Night* (1962); *The Long Walk Home* (1990).

HEBREWS 5:12—6:1, 9-12 (23rd Sunday/Proper 25)

In this pericope Hebrews chides its readers with remaining stuck in the elementary aspects of Christian faith. The writer would like to offer them "solid food," but he is compelled to settle for "the milk" of elementary Christian teaching, which he fears they have forgotten (cf. 1 Cor. 3:1-3). He regrets that he must once more remind them of the basic teaching about Christ, the foundation of repentance and faith.

Hebrews appeals to an earlier devotion of his audience in serving one another, an ardor that has died down and is in danger of eclipse (6:10). The writer's approach is to acknowledge a former commitment well expressed in community, a commitment that he still recognizes in some persons in his audience. What he appeals for is "the same diligence" on the part of the whole community he addresses (6:11). He points to "sluggishness" as the imminent danger for those who fail to value the promise of salvation in Christ, and he summons them to be "imitators" of those who by faith and patience have gained the promise (6:12). This same theme is elaborately developed later in a lengthy recital of Old Testament faithful from Abraham to the prophets, culminating in Jesus himself, as models of persistence in faith, worthy to be emulated (11:1—12:2).

What attitudes and behaviors in his audience are referred to by their preference for "milk" over "solid food"? It seems to refer to their wanting to hear over and over about their salvation, while shirking the hard challenges of consistent Christian behavior and the tasks of service in the church. They are happy to carry out rituals of cleansing and laying on of hands, and they are pleased at words about resurrection and eternal judgment (6:2). Yet in spite of their involvement in rites and teachings, they hang back in an infantile stage of faith instead of advancing toward maturity. They still are content "to be taught," when by now they should be "teaching" others. Why this lethargy? The problem seems to be that they are demoralized and dispirited by the opposition they face from without and by fearfulness and withdrawal from full commitment to one another within.

If the writer could give them "solid food," what would it be? Apparently it would be precisely what he is telling them by writing as he does, but he fears that they will not be able to receive what he has to say. He wants them to understand the incredible resources of salvation in Christ and the large responsibilities placed on those who receive the benefits of Jesus. He wants them to see that faith will not exempt them from hardship, which if faced courageously, will strengthen them beyond measure. He is trying with all the rhetorical appeals he can muster to ground them in renewed confidence and energize them to renewed commitment that will endure. He is telling them that just as it was costly for Jesus to accomplish their salvation, so it will be costly for them to live out their salvation.

How does one preach such themes in a mode that is not a "put on a happy face" pep talk or a browbeating harangue? The answer may be to follow the mode of Hebrews and point to the benefits of growing up in faith in contrast to the dangers of remaining stuck with a childish faith. The strategy of Hebrews is to identify the "sore points" of faithlessness in his readers, the symptoms of their malaise, and to probe for the root causes. In what respects are we Christians adrift and dispirited these days? Here we need to be as honest and specific as possible about our congregational life and about the way we approach our daily lives and the outlook we have upon the larger world. Do we actually understand that claiming Christ is a big commitment, lifelong and far-reaching in its implications and effects? What work of restoration and renewal do we need to do? What further steps do we need to take as individuals and as corporate bodies? What is needed to bring joy and satisfaction to our Christian calling?

For motivation in this enterprise of faith renewal, Hebrews proposes that we look intently at Jesus and those who preceded him in the faith. The writer says that because Jesus not only preceded us, but also stands beside us, we too can live a life of unfolding faith sufficient to each stage and situation of life. At this point, a sermon might well call for a look at those who have followed Jesus over the centuries since Hebrews wrote. In particular, we can think of "a roll call of the faithful" in our immediate experience as believers and as congregations. Who do we know who exhibits the qualities we aspire to, so that they are tangible and conceivable for us? It is all well and good that the Bible seems to be full of such folk, although we probably exaggerate their virtues. Do we see those qualities and commitments in people today, and do we find them corporately expressed inside and outside the church? Where are these present pioneers of faith? If it seems to ask a great deal of us to live that way, what happens to us as persons, congregations, communities, societies if we do not so live? Has Jesus our high priest triumphed on earth and in heaven, only to be without a present following on earth?

Movies: *The Fixer* (1968); *Sounder* (1972).

HEBREWS 7:23-28 (24th Sunday/Proper 26)

This portion of Hebrews "hammers away" at the absolute superiority of Jesus' high priesthood over the priestly functionaries of the Old Testament order. We have already encountered the observation that the priests of the old order had to offer sacrifice for their own sins as well as for those of the laity. To this limitation, the author now adds that there were necessarily many priests, who because of their finitude, succeeded one another. The office of the priest endured, but particular priests came and went. The decisive difference with Jesus is that "he holds his priesthood permanently." The text again cites Psalm 110 and the priest Melchizedek who rules forever as perfectly consummated in Jesus. A cunning piece of exegesis notes that the oath to Melchizedek, appearing in a psalm of David, comes *later* than the law of Moses, and thus has priority over the earlier Mosaic priesthood (v. 28). By contrast, Paul argued that the justification of Abraham's faith, coming *earlier* than Mosaic law, was superior to justification by keeping the law (Gal. 3:17).

This is surely one of the most "otherworldly" passages in Hebrews. From our perspective, it replaces the lived world of change and impermanence with the higher world of eternity. Jesus appears elevated to a status that is beyond our comprehension. He is said to be "perfect forever" (v. 28). The oppositions here are between transitoriness, weakness, and ineffectuality, on the one hand, and permanence, strength, and effectuality, on the other. Thus, Jesus appears vastly removed from humankind and the changefulness of our lives in history seems of little consequence. In appearing to assign all merit and value to heaven and all demerit and valuelessness to earth, we are tempted to feel like hopelessly passive recipients of blessings from a distant deity. If we had only this passage in isolation from the rest of Hebrews, we might well set it aside as grievously misleading for Christians today.

In the larger argument of Hebrews, however, we observe a deliberate disruption of this dualistic worldview, when it is asserted again and again that Jesus attained his high status of "perfection" by living a stressful human life, subject to all the forces that play upon human beings, while remaining firm and consistent in his mission. He is perfect high priest not because he belongs solely and splendidly to the eternal world above, but because he was "promoted" to high priesthood precisely as a consequence of being a fully faithful human being on earth. His perfection is not a divine state of flawlessness simply accorded him without effort; it is an achievement—even a prize—of faithfulness over the course of his life that he has run as a race is run (12:1-2).

Just as Job's "perfection" was the attainment of an undivided heart toward God, so Jesus's "perfection" is the summing up of the life he lived in faithful communion with God. And just as Job's "perfection" allowed of anger, impatience, and despair, so the "perfection" of Jesus embraced his anger, impatience, and despair (see the Job texts below). He was perfect not because he was immune to human temptations and vices—but because he did not turn from his calling in spite of all the forces without and within that urged him to do so.

The writer of Hebrews is struggling with two schemes of thought that don't quite "gel," a transcendental-idealist perspective and a historical-eschatological perspective. Thus Hebrews offers one way—far from the only way—of acclaiming Jesus' achievement by emphasizing its end result in predominantly otherworldly imagery. But the truth is that there would have been no occasion for a Christian writer to invoke this otherworldly window dressing had not Jesus in his actual life followed his calling and achieved a victory over sin and death in a manner diametrically opposed to the overall Platonic view of the superior world of ideas sharply set off from the inferior world of the flesh. The Jewish apocalyptic mode of counterposing heaven and earth is somewhat more congenial to the thrust of Hebrews since it allows that the struggle of the faithful on earth has an impact on heavenly decisions.

A sermon preachable on this passage might illuminate how we Christians have used various images and schemes of thought to talk about how and why Jesus came to be our Savior and Lord. No one image or scheme has been satisfactory to all believers. The nub of our devotion is connected

with the very earthly life of Jesus lived faithfully through and beyond
death. While we necessarily employ images and schemes of thought available to us, we want to be careful not to straitjacket Jesus within them. We
may rather want to let Jesus and our experience of him confront the very
images and schemes we use to explain him—and in the process to evaluate
and transform them. Jesus forever escapes us, as he forever ministers to us
and leads us. Is not this his "perfection," that he repeatedly validates himself to us as the master interpreter of life and the deliverer from its snares
and delusions? So we may thank Hebrews for its ingenious rendering of
the triumph of Jesus, but it will not replace other renderings, either in the
New Testament or in our own hearts and minds.

   Movies: *Jesus of Montreal* (1989); *The Last Temptation of Christ*
(1988).

HEBREWS 9:11-14 (24th Sunday/Proper 26)
HEBREWS 9:24-28 (25th Sunday/Proper 27)

In this segment of Hebrews, the author provides his most extensive elabo-
ration of the continuities and discontinuities between the Old Testament
sacrificial cult and the sacrifice of Christ. Previously, an explicit connection and contrast was drawn between "the sanctuary and true tent" in the
heavens (8:2) and the earthly Israelite tent as "a copy and shadow of the
heavenly sanctuary" (8:5). In making this point, Hebrews cites Exod. 25:9,
40 where it is said that the tent and its furnishings are to be built "according to the pattern" shown to Moses "on the mountain." The structural blue-
print revealed to Moses is viewed by our author as modeled on the true
heavenly sanctuary.

   At this point Hebrews sets forth the cultic arrangements of the Old Testament tent in line with Exodus 25–31, noting in particular an innermost
sanctuary where the high priest alone enters to offer blood sacrifices on the
Day of Atonement. This sets the stage for a peroration on Christ as high
priest who enters "the perfect tent" in the heavens and offers his own
blood. The tent of the old covenant was made with human hands, and the
blood of the old covenant was the blood of animals. The superiority of the
new covenant "tent" consists in its construction by God, and the superiority of the new covenant sacrifice consists in its being the freely offered
blood of Christ himself. If the sacrifices of old had a partial and limited
efficacy, "how much more" does the sacrifice of the Son assure the purification of believers.

   In the course of the argument, Hebrews makes much of the sacrificial
blood that ratified the old covenant, being sprinkled on the people and on

the tent and its furnishings. But this singular blood rite performed by Moses at the sealing of the covenant was not sufficient since the high priest had to perform atoning blood rites annually within the sanctuary. In contrast, the singular sacrifice of Christ at the ratification of the new covenant renders unnecessary any further sacrificial actions because the blood of his sacrifice was his own and its effect is "once for all" (v. 26).

The prominence of the blood imagery can be easily misconstrued as magic, as if the physical blood of animals and of Jesus are in and of themselves agents with cleansing properties. It is the life given up fully to God that counts for redemption, of which "blood" is the compressed symbol. If the blood symbolism is reduced to material magic, a grotesque image results of the ascendent Christ offering the physical blood of the historical Jesus within the heavenly sanctuary. When Hebrews says that Christ now appears "in the presence of God on our behalf" (v. 24), what he presents on behalf of humans is not a vessel of blood but his own faithfulness to God in life and death as the obedient perfected Son. And although the sacrifice of Christ is singular and complete, not needing to be repeated because the historical life and death of Jesus is not repeatable, the atoning activity of Christ never ends, as is sharply articulated by the author in these words, "Consequently he is able for all time to save those who approach God through him, since he always lives to make intercession for them" (7:25).

This grandiose vision, relentlessly advancing its complex cultic imagery, exposes more of the logical and ethical difficulties that follow from adopting either the Platonic idealist philosophy or the apocalyptic notion of the two worlds. Here the time of the historical Jesus is intertwined with the eternality of the ascendent Christ in ways that simply cannot be literalized. If we isolate or separate particular features of the imagery, we easily fall into absurdities that the author himself, were he with us, would likely disown. Moreover, when the Platonic/apocalyptic schemes that shape the discourse of Hebrews are joined with current popular notions of a sharp split between material and spiritual reality, it is no wonder that the book feels more often like an enigma to be unraveled than the practical encouragement it was intended to be. By fixing on bits and pieces of the argument it has been possible for some interpreters to miss the dynamic movement of salvation that Hebrews strives to trace. Reinforced by tendencies in the interpreters' cultural and religious environment, this may lead to a sole focus on the bloody death of Jesus or to a totally spiritualized notion of Christian faith—in disregard of the full scope of the epistle.

A homiletical approach to this complex imagery of salvation might best regard the book not as a formal theological discourse but as an imaginative reflection on the liturgy, or living worship, of Christian existence. It sets forth the interior meaning of our worship as the believers' risky self-giving in the light of the self-giving of Jesus, a self-giving so efficacious that it cancels out sin and motivates abiding faith among those who adhere to him and his pattern of life. This accords well with the exhortations to emulate the steadfast trust of Jesus in his obedience to God.

Hebrews thus dwells on the turning points in life, the moments of stress and crisis, when we stand "on the threshold" of change. These moments in individual and communal life are occasions either to fall back into old established ways, or to go forward into new as-yet-uncertain possibilities (10:39). Under varied images, such as "entering into rest" and "running the race set before us," Hebrews points to this crisis-laden open-ended course of life. It is the reality discerned by anthropology in the rites of passage surrounding such liminal (threshold) situations as birth, puberty, marriage, and death—all fraught with social psychological and religious significance.

Viewed in this way, the epistle may speak convincingly to us as a vivid dramatization of the high stakes we face at various critical junctures in our changeful existence, as it also invokes the rich resources available along the pathway that Jesus Christ opens up for us—access to God and faithful living with others. The sermonic challenge would be to identify and portray the points where we are under stress today, either "to give up" or "to go on" growing. What are the ideas and behaviors that either "pull us back" and "weigh us down" or "spur us forward" and "lift us up"? What are the challenges and tests facing this congregation at this moment in our corporate life? How can our stated worship each Sunday, so easily mired in unthinking routine, be shaped and offered so that it sets forth the precarious joyful venture of the Christian life? How can our worship become a vehicle for the grace and judgment of the living God addressing us in the life-giving Son?

Movies: *Dead Man Walking* (1996); *Matewan* (1987).

HEBREWS 10:11-25, 31-39 (26th Sunday/Proper 28)

Our author's lengthy and resourceful employment of the high priestly imagery of Jesus, played out in close dialogue with its Old Testament analogues, comes to its climax in this section. The book throughout has alternated expositions of the high priestly functions of Christ with exhortations that flow from the exposition. Now the author is poised for his final, more extended and detailed appeals, which give the impression of being addressed to a particular community and its special problems.

The challenge before the author appears to be this: How are we to connect the absolute sufficiency and finality of the salvation offered us by

Christ with our own fragility and fickleness in claiming and adhering to this salvation? Or, put another way, although salvation in Christ is eternally available, our own lives in time being tumultuous and episodic, how do we keep a hold on a timeless salvation? Or, again, since the purification from sins is solely the work of Jesus Christ, is there really anything required of us in order to access and appropriate the purifying redemption he has effected? In short, the awkwardness we feel in the heaven/earth dualism of Hebrews, which does not constitute a conceptual problem for the author, does eventually emerge for him as a practical pastoral problem, precisely because of the tensions that Christians experience when they try to live on earth as though heaven were present. In his theological argument, the writer of Hebrews has opened a wide gulf between heaven and earth that he now attempts to narrow in his exhortations to Christian living.

The resolution to this dilemma, as Hebrews sees it, lies in the way Jesus Christ "bridges" the gap between our earthly lives and the heavenly resources of salvation. He bridged that gap once decisively in his earthly existence, and he continually bridges it in his heavenly existence. He knows our weaknesses and struggles at all of life's thresholds because he has experienced them. He simultaneously opens up for us a "vertical" access to God and clears for us a "horizontal" pathway into and through life's difficulties. So the "theological" rendering of the work of Jesus is elegantly clear, but how helpful was this way of viewing Jesus for its original recipients and how helpful is it for us?

That the enormously powerful salvific effects of Jesus Christ might be misconstrued as a kind of magic, an inevitable result of claiming them in a formal manner, appears to be a possible grave misunderstanding for the recipients of Hebrews and for us. It is not enough to have made a confession of Christ and joined the church. One must "hold on" to one's confession of faith. For Hebrews, faith is not so much the initial act of confessing Christ (as in Acts), or being in close communion with Christ (as in Paul), as it is the confidence in Christ that endures through all obstacles. This "full assurance of faith" is demonstrated in our ever-renewed readiness to approach him in complete confidence that we will find grace and power "to keep on keeping on." The imagery of the heavenly sanctuary, previously focused on its counterpart in the Israelite tent and on Christ's triumphant entry therein, is now pictured as the space where we can enter to renew constantly our trust and courage.

This is no mere image or abstraction. The author sketches some of the threshold challenges that his audience has had to face and may yet be facing. In the past, perhaps not a distant past, they have suffered opposition that included confiscation of their property and imprisonment for some.

These painful losses and restrictions did not disperse their community or totally destroy its faith (vv. 32-34). Yet it was demoralizing. Some may have left the church altogether. Others have neglected to meet together (v. 25). The result appears to be a church that has grown fearful and irresolute in its faith and practice. The author means to say to them: You do not understand what I am saying to you about the saving power of Jesus Christ unless you dare to take all your hardships and fears into the presence of Christ who overcame his hardships and fears and allow his forgiveness to empower you amid your most pressing difficulties.

In a sense, Hebrew appears to claim that Christ purifies from all sin except the sin of refusing to act as though we are truly purified. "It is a fearful thing to fall into the hands of the living God" (10:31), a declamation so loved by Jonathan Edwards, comes initially as a shock. But in every "today," says Hebrews, we may "harken to the voice" of the one who purifies, or we may "harden our hearts." The author does not try to define any precise point at which we may forfeit our faith irrevocably, but he firmly believes that Christians—however sincere their confession—may be lost to the efficacy of the heavenly high priest because of subsequent faithlessness. He fears that those he addresses are flirting with just such a grievous loss. Yet he has hope: "But we are not among those who shrink back and are lost, but among those who have faith and are saved" (v. 39).

What can be preached about this text without being tediously moralizing? How can the preacher preach to her/himself while preaching to others? How can the church internalize this message as a reminder that our faith is not an escape or a dodge from the hardships of life—both those that we cannot avoid and those that come to us because we elect to take risks for what we take to be God's leading? Have we, in this congregation, grown lethargic and weary, or perhaps smug and self-assured, no longer addressing real issues in our daily lives and in our community and nation? It does not seem that sermons alone, or any number of epistles like Hebrews, will suffice unless we note another counsel in this pericope, "let us consider how to provoke one another to love and good deeds . . . encouraging one another" (vv. 24-25). Do our assemblies, programs, and activities stimulate and encourage one another to live out corporately and individually the saving effects of our high priest, who is likewise "the pioneer and perfecter of our faith" (12:2)? How do we get beneath our church routines and shake them up so that we enable love and good deeds to flourish? Does not the sharing of the priestly work of Christ fall upon all of us as merciful and empowering priests to one another?

Movies: *Cries and Whispers* (1972); *La Strada* (1954).

The Pathway through Torah, Poetry, Prophecy, Wisdom, and Apocalyptic

The Old Testament texts commented on below are related to particular Gospel and epistle texts in the cycle of lectionary readings. In many cases the connections between the Old Testament and New Testament readings are evident in direct citation or in similarity of theme, but in some cases the presumed links are more difficult to discern. Two texts from the New Testament, Mark 13 and Revelation 1, are included here because of their genre and thematic links with Daniel.

I. A Torah Text

DEUTERONOMY 6:1-9 (24th Sunday/Proper 26)

This is a foundational text for Judaism in the late biblical period and down to the present. It is called the *Shema*, after the first word of Deut. 6:4, "Hear, O Israel!" It is recited in a text written some time in the seventh–sixth century B.C.E. The *Shema* calls for unqualified love of God with our whole being. It further stipulates that love of God is to be demonstrated by keeping the laws set forth in the totality of the book of Deuteronomy. Particular emphasis is placed on inculcating these laws in the routine of daily life. Children are to be taught them within the context of family life.

The command to love God, supplemented by love of neighbor (drawn from Lev. 19:18), served as an epitome of the numerous laws within the one Torah. Jesus so regarded them, along with other Jews of his time (see Mark 12:28-34). There was, however, a great variety of interpretations of these laws during the lifetime of Jesus. Contrary to the stricter views of certain Jews, such as the Pharisees, Jesus showed considerable flexibility in his interpretation of particular laws and customs associated with the laws, such that he felt free to evaluate them in terms of their effects on people and their appropriateness in meeting immediate human needs.

In no case, however, does Jesus totally abrogate the law, but works within it, beneath it, and beyond it to stress the sovereign presence of God in human life. For him, the law sometimes seems a sufficient vehicle to express the love of God. At other times, particular laws within the law might be set aside in favor of some higher good. This situational freedom of Jesus toward the law served as a model for early Christianity which set aside the cultic laws of the Torah while retaining its substance for ethical and spiritual instruction. While all Christians can readily agree on love of

God and neighbor as a central feature of their faith, the ways that love is to be shown have been much disputed and its actual expression, particularly to obnoxious "neighbors"—not to mention "aliens" who are likewise to be loved (Lev. 19:34)—has been partial at best.

A sermon on this text could profitably explore the summons "to recite" these words at home and "to talk about them" in company with our children. Does the congregation to whom we minister have substantial lay biblical instruction to equip members to study the Bible on their own? Do we have adequate education programs that take into account child development and appropriate ways to share biblical faith with the young at their various stages of growth? What practical resources do we offer our members in this area of family religious education?

Movies: *The Chosen* (1981); *The Hiding Place* (1975).

II. Poetic and Prophetic Texts

I SAMUEL 2:1-10 (26th Sunday/Proper 28)

This thanksgiving song is put on the lips of the long-barren Hannah after she gave birth to Samuel and dedicated him to temple service (1 Samuel 1). It is a song that celebrates radical reversals in the fortunes of various types of people, for good and ill. All these changes of fortune are presented as the work of Yahweh who intervenes on behalf of the poor and needy and abases the arrogant mighty ones. This text is best known to Christian Bible readers through its quotation in the Magnificat of Mary (Luke 1:52-53).

In its present form, the song appears to have been adapted for use in the royal cult since it closes with a promise of strength to the Israelite king (v. 10) who is probably to be pictured as the speaker of v. 1. The appropriateness of this song for the lowly Israelite woman Hannah was probably suggested by the reference to the barren woman who marvelously bears children (v. 5). When we consider class and power positions, there is a great gulf between Hannah and the Israelite king. The song's theme of social redemption for the poor and needy is ironically spoken by the king, for it is he who wields the very power under which the poor and needy so often suffer. There is thus a prophetic thrust to the song that overtakes and questions all those who would use it from a position of power over other people. Precisely this is the tenor of its incorporation into Mary's Magnificat, which as whole seems to have been modeled on the Song of Hannah.

The most obvious sermon here is about the precarious moral position of all in positions of power in church and society. Since power so easily justifies itself, there is a continual question—pointed like an arrow—at those who exercise it: Is our exercise of power "raising up the poor" and "lifting up the needy"? Or are we "talking so very proudly" while exploiting and manipulating those we ostensibly serve? What are some of the ways that church leadership, and the church's own prestigious position in society, become abusive and therefore contrary to God's desire to empower all God's people?

Movies: *In the Name of the Father* (1993); *The Shawshank Redemption* (1994).

2 SAMUEL 23:1-7 (Christ the King Sunday/Proper 29)

This song about just kingship is introduced as "the last words of David," cast in a prophetic style and called "an oracle." It is a song that aims to give theological and moral legitimacy to the ongoing dynasty of David that endured for over four hundred years until the destruction of Jerusalem in 587 B.C.E. Biblical traditions show, however, that the Davidic dynasty was contested even in his lifetime, and certainly by the Northern Kingdom which broke away after the death of Solomon. Moreover, prophets brought serious charges against later Davidic rulers and in some instances even prophesied the destruction of the dynasty.

The central claim of the song is that "one who rules over people justly" merits "an everlasting covenant" such as the one made by God with David and his descendants (2 Samuel 7). Nevertheless, the song features an ambivalence in that David does not directly claim just rule but asks, "Is not my house like this with God?" Granted that the question is rhetorical, with David expecting the answer, "Yes, of course." Nevertheless, a space is left for "no," or "maybe." That the text pushes this query to the forefront indicates that the dynasty felt required to justify itself on religious grounds.

The central image of the song is the king symbolized by the bright sun that causes the earth to sprout forth after rain. The "grass" as stand-in for all life-giving plants typifies the blessed lives of the righteous subjects of the king. By contrast, "the godless," those who resist the king—whether northern monarchs or Judahite subjects—are like "thorns," dangerous to handle and worthy only to be consumed by fire.

As with the Song of Hannah, we are here confronted with strong claims of leaders concerning their just rule that invite careful scrutiny. Political ideology reinforced by religious ideology, fixing on inflammatory popular themes of being "godly," "patriotic," "pro-family," "budget-balancing," and so forth, necessitate careful Christian discernment. What are the actual values and programs that go under the cover of these religious claims? What is the whole effect of this leadership on all sectors of the population? Who benefits and who is hurt or neglected by their way of conceiving and administrating government? The prophetic passages below provide some clues as to the criteria by which we may evaluate high-sounding claims of leaders to govern in the name of God and on behalf of the real needs of people.

Movies: *All the King's Men* (1949); *Bob Roberts* (1992).

AMOS 5:6-7, 10-15 (21st Sunday/Proper 23)

Two excerpts from the blistering oracles of Amos address the upper classes in northern Israel in the mid-eighth century. From the perspective of Amos, in breaking away from the inequities of the Davidic dynasty, the north has fallen into similar, if not worse, injustices.

The first excerpt (vv. 6-7) pronounces judgment on Bethel, which was one of the northern royal sanctuaries. All the accoutrements and symbols of power and wealth are concentrated on such a site. The text has just enjoined people not to take part in the cult at Bethel (5:5), so outrageously hypocritical is it in its consumption of goods and its inducement to self-righteousness in the face of poverty and injustice perpetrated by those who flock to worship.

Amos highlights two interconnected practices among "the many transgressions" and "great sins" of his audience. The first "sin" is taking levies or exactions of grain from the small farmers that made up the bulk of the populace (v. 11). These forced extractions from their livelihood came in two forms: one was in exorbitant taxation by the state, and the other was in onerous interest on loans made to the small farmers, eventuating in foreclosed mortgages, debt slavery, and loss of property. The second "sin," which served to gloss over the first, is corruption of the judicial system through bribery and intimidation (v. 12). Ordinary folks who brought complaints against big landholders and merchants stood little chance of a hearing. It was typical for the powerful "to purchase" a judgment in their favor by outright bribery or by threats of extralegal reprisal.

The prophet speaks of these abusive treatments of commoners in strong bodily imagery. The abusers are said to "trample on the poor" and "push aside the needy" (vv. 11-12). In Amos 2:7 this trampling on the heads of the poor is described even more forcefully as a "pulverizing" of the poor into dust. Isaiah puts this horror in the form of an accusatory question addressed by God to the elders and princes: "What do you mean by crushing my people, by grinding the face of the poor?" (3:15).

Why do so many churches pass over these strictures on the brutalization of the socially weak? How is that so many businessmen and politicians reared in the church have so little sense of social justice? This would be a worthy topic for reflection in a sermon on Amos. A number of factors come to mind that combine in subtle ways to devalue social justice in the priorities of church members. We are under the spell of the innocence of the American economic system that is allegedly good for everybody—if not now, at least some day when it gets finer tuned. We are mesmerized by a personalized piety that does not encourage us to look beyond self and family. We are affected by a belief that success is a sign of virtue and blessing by God. Thus, if we are among the big "winners" of power and wealth we are assured that we are good people, and if we are among the big "losers" we are shamed into believing that it is our own fault.

Another reason that social justice gets short shrift in our churches is that its multiple causes and effects are complicated to trace in all detail. It is very easy to deliver a sermon on Amos full of sweeping generalizations that elicits routine nods and some grumbling, and little more. It is also to be noted that the fiercest words of Amos are directed to the high-level leaders who control power and set the tone of society. Often the churches we serve have few such persons among their members. So our sermonizing, as well as the resolutions passed by congregations and church bodies, needs to take account of levels of power and responsibility on social justice matters. The biblical demands of social justice come in different shapes according to the positions we hold in society.

Movies: *The Field* (1990); *Norma Rae* (1979).

JEREMIAH 31:7-9 (23rd Sunday/Proper 25)

This sample of prophetic verse comes from the so-called Book of Consolation, Jeremiah 30–31, in which the redemption and return of Israel after exile are celebrated in a series of songs full of comfort and promise. The reason for including it in association with Mark 10:46-52 appears to be the occurrence of blindness in both passages. In the latter, blind Bartimaeus is healed. In the Jeremiah text, among the returnees to Judah will be "the blind and the lame, those with child and those in labor." In Jeremiah and Mark, the blindness is literal, whereas in many biblical passages "blindness" is a metaphor for confusion, incomprehension, and faithlessness (see Isa. 59:9-19). The aim in mentioning these weak and vulnerable members among the returning exiles is to stress God's care for all, toward whom God is a solicitous nurturing "father." Such divine care for the weakest could be the emphasis of a sermon on this text, or, alternatively, it could be used with other biblical passages on blindness to elucidate the Markan text.

Movies: *Exodus* (1960); *Yellow Submarine* (1968).

ISAIAH 53:4-12 (22nd Sunday/Proper 24)

Surely one of the top Christian "favorites" among Old Testament texts, this thanksgiving song, enclosing a lament, tells of the undeserved oppression of a faithful servant of God who is delivered from the clutches of death and vindicated by a return to favor in the community that once despised him. This text is explicitly applied to Jesus in parts of the New Testament (e.g., Acts 8:26-40), and is thought by many interpreters to be the background for the Markan reference to the Son of Man as one who gives his life as "a ransom for many" (10:45). Unfortunately, the lectionary cuts off the first fourth of the song, which should be read beginning at 52:13 for full effect.

The two major competing identities attributed to the servant are either that he is a personification of Israel in exile or that he is some person in Israel's past history or a living person known to the prophet. A close look at the text suggests that we have here a thanksgiving song encompassing a lament concerning a leader in the exile. This anonymous person was falsely delivered to judgment and a sentence of death from which he was snatched and returned to the community that had formerly disowned him but now embraced him and his mission. The impression that the servant had actually died and was resurrected is probably mistaken, since the song follows typical imagery of the Psalms in which the extreme plight of a sufferer is described as though he had entered into the realm of death, from which God plucks him at the last moment (cf. Pss. 9:13; 22:15; 31:12; 69:14-15; 71:20; 88:4-6; 143:3).

God speaks of the servant in laudatory terms at the beginning of the song (52:13-15) and at the end (53:11b-12). The body of the text is a lament over the persecution, trial, and delivery to death of the servant. The unnamed "we" who lament also confess their complicity in his sufferings and acknowledge that in some sense he suffered for their sins. This anonymous "we" is probably the exilic community that "sacrificed" the servant by turning him over to Babylonian authorities. A credible hypothesis is that the servant is the prophet who wrote Isaiah 40–55, the one whose speeches and writings openly encouraged the exiles to prepare for return to their homeland once their present overlords, the Babylonians, are defeated by Cyrus the Persian. At the very verge of execution, the prophet escapes or is released and his former tormentors now acclaim him as one who has opened their eyes to the correctness of the prophet's mission.

This rendering of the identity of the servant and of the circumstances surrounding his oppression and vindication brings the portrait of the servant into close proximity to the opposition suffered by Jeremiah some decades earlier and to the trial and death of Jesus some centuries later. Both were politically persecuted on charges of sedition against the state that carried strong religious overtones. Jeremiah escaped death because he had highly placed sympathizers and advocates who helped to spare him. Jesus had no such sympathizers or advocates with enough power to thwart the complicity of Jewish and Roman authorities in putting him to death. All three figures are examples of those with a strongly felt mission from God that threatens established political and religious structures—a mission that they pursue even to the point of their death. All three, though largely deserted by their contemporaries, were subsequently vindicated in the eyes of many who had formerly scorned them.

The remaining feature in the text to be considered is the claim that the servant suffered the punishment that belonged to his betrayers and in his self-offering "healed the transgressions and iniquities" of which they were guilty (v. 5). The servant is even said to have "made himself an offering for sin" (v. 10). This introduces notions of sacrifice for sin that appear in various guises throughout the Bible (see Heb. 7:23-28). One common way to think of this action is to regard it as a vicarious or substitutionary atonement, in which the voluntary sufferer "takes the hit" of punishment from God that was due to guilty sinners, thereby freeing them from the just penalty for their wrongs. This has been an appealing way for many Christians to make sense of the saving death of Jesus. It has, however, seemed less than satisfactory to numerous other Christians, even grotesque when carried to its extreme. Its tendency is to make of Jesus "a scapegoat" who magically removes our sins through a sweeping juridical act of God, without necessarily involving us in any other way than to assent to this arbitrary gift.

There is another way of comprehending this "sacrifice" that both respects the initiative of God and the intrinsic involvement of the human beneficiaries. To begin with, all these sufferers voluntarily choose the course of action that propels them into conflict. It is their mission to represent the life-giving and life-sustaining resources of God for establishing true community. In pursing their mission, they clash with the old structures of death, and in their faithfulness to the new order of life, their suffering and willingness to die (and even their actual death, as with Jesus) has a life-renewing impact on others. Far from a legal enactment, this self-giving of God's servants changes lives and empowers communities. Only some such historical and ethical reading of sacrificial suffering and death seems adequate to explain the ministry of Jesus and his teaching to his disciples, as typified in the accompanying Gospel reading (Mark 10:35-45). For Jesus, the sign that his disciples have understood his role in their lives is not that they now feel free to go their own way because he has released them from God's punishment. The sign that they truly know him is that, now free from the domination of sin, they are drawn into Jesus' servant pattern of life—in which they too may have to suffer, but this time not because of their stupidity and weakness but because of their conversion to his way of servant-hood. Indeed, we can think of this as a radical alternative version of "substitutionary atonement." It is not that "deserved punishment" is replaced by the substitute of "freedom from consequences." Instead, we find that "compulsive bondage to self" is replaced by the substitution of "free servanthood with Christ."

A sermon on this text is an opportunity to explore the ways that the self-giving of God's servants, and supremely Jesus, elicits self-giving from others. In doing so, we need to examine closely what we expect in the way of self-giving service from ourselves and others. It has been typical for church folk whose status is devalued in society—such as women, the poor, and the uneducated—to hear the call to sacrificial service as a call to more self-effacement. They may embrace the call in an attempt to acquire some substitute status, or they may reject it resentfully. Meanwhile, those with greater status and power are inclined to think the call to service a bit excessive and certainly inconvenient to their accustomed social standards. We should be cautious in asking any one other than ourselves "to sacrifice."

Movies: *Nazarin* (1958); *Romero* (1989).

ISAIAH 59:9-19 (23rd Sunday/Proper 25)

This passage speaks from the situation of the returnees to Palestine and it is much concerned with lapses in faith and practice among the Jews living in restored Judah. The reading is in two parts: a lament and confession (vv. 9-15a) and a theophany of divine judgment and purgation (vv. 15b-20). The topics of concern in the two sections are dissimilar, and should be sharply distinguished. A better division is to take 59:1-15a as an integral unit, quite separable from the remainder of the chapter.

The topic that runs throughout 59:1-15a is the dearth of justice and righteousness in the community. The passage starts as a prophetic judgment speech. In the assigned portion of the text, a lament breaks out in a "we" voice that eventually turns into a confession of sins. Thus, in the lament, the preceding indictment is accepted and internalized by some group within Judah. The disruptions of community include murder and lying, and what looks like factional struggles of the sort mentioned elsewhere in Isaiah 55–66. There are colorful images of communal drift and disorder: people grope like the blind along a wall, stumble like the walking dead, growl at one another like bears and mourn like doves. The "we" who acknowledge the truth of the prophetic indictment are not, however, numerous or powerful enough to change the overall dismal communal situation.

The simile of blindness (v. 10) appears to have been the reason for grouping this text with the healing of Bartimaeus' blindness in Mark 10:46-52. A sermon could be developed on symptoms of communal disorder and breakdown. Rather similar laments are regularly raised about the state of American society these days. In what respects are we groping blind, walking dead, growling bears, and mourning doves? A twist worth introducing is the situation of a group of people (the "we" of the lament) who own up to their part in the general social breakdown but who don't seem to be able to make much difference. If we feel some affinity with them today, our lament and confession may be a helpful first step, better than indifference or denying involvement. But what next? Many Christians are seeking further steps. Where should we be directing our efforts and with what analyses and expectations? The deceptive goal of making this "a Christian nation" is grandiose, and is often pursued with an incredible self-righteousness toward non-Christians and Christians with differing views, as well as exhibiting shallow understandings of serious social problems. What is a wiser, more modest, goal that can honestly address urgent problems and heal festering divisions?

Movies: *Germinal* (1993); *A World Apart* (1988).

III. Wisdom Texts

JOB 1:1; 2:1-10 (20th Sunday/Proper 22)

This is the first of four excerpts from Job offered as alternate readings in the Revised Common Lectionary. This pericope, and part of the last reading from Job, are stories and strictly speaking belong in our narrative pathway. However, because the narrative of Job is used as a frame for the brilliant poetic speeches in the body of the work, we have chosen to treat the narrative and the speeches together as aspects of an integral piece of wisdom literature.

This portion from the prologue of Job recounts part of the familiar story of a "blameless and upright" man of wealth and status who came upon evil days. His loss of property and children, and his grievous skin disease, are pictured as instigated by a celestial Accuser and permitted by God as a test of the integrity of his faith. Job accepts these horrible reversals of fortune without complaint. When chided by his wife for his unnatural composure and resignation (is she saying, in effect, "Be honest, Job!"), he rebukes her and declaims that the good and bad alike should be received from God without protest.

Questions immediately arise regarding the person of the Accuser, the action of God in permitting Job's affliction, and the reserved compliant response of the sufferer. The Hebrew word for the Accuser, *ha-satan*, is not a proper name but the description of an office, the role of master spy among the "sons of God" in the divine assembly, a figure appearing elsewhere in the Old Testament only in Zech. 3:1-2 and 1 Chron. 21:1. The exchange between the Accuser and God is dressed in the mythology of the divine assembly where God presides as cosmic ruler surrounded by courtly attendants. The Accuser's assignment is to patrol the earth with an eye for evildoers. God "asks for trouble" by calling the Accuser's attention to Job, the most righteous of all men, as if to force the Accuser to concur. The Accuser replies that Job only appears to be perfect because God has treated him so bountifully. If faced with adversity, Job will assuredly curse God. In agreeing to allow the Accuser to afflict Job, God takes up the dare implicit in the accusation that Job's piety is shallow and ephemeral.

Oddly enough, although we readers are informed of it, this heavenly wager is unknown to all the human characters in the book of Job. Even when God finally speaks to Job at the end of the book, not a word is said about the wager between the deity and one of the heavenly attendants. As a result, this mythic dramatization of the notion that suffering is intended to test faith appears as only one of several views of the source of suffering that emerge in the fierce disputes between Job and his friends. To the very end, Job lacks the master key to his situation that the prologue supplies. We wonder about the intent of the author in giving us an explanation that is withheld from the principals in the story. Does the book of Job, apparently from several hands, intend to privilege the heavenly wager as the true explanation of Job's plight? Or is this bold theological explanation bracketed as an example of the inscrutability of suffering which, as far as we humans are concerned, can never be adequately explained? Or does the heavenly wager imply that, without knowing it, Job actually did "pass the test" by remaining faithful to God even when he railed against God?

The exchange in the divine assembly reveals a resourceful Accuser and an insecure God who is not really sure of Job's faith once a doubt has been raised. We witness deity capitulating to the temptation to disbelieve the deity's own best servant on earth. God here is vulnerable to a temptation very like the snare that entrapped Eve. "Did God really say . . . ?" inquires the serpent of Eve. "Does Job really fear God without reason?" asks the Accuser. Both questions insinuate a negative reply without requiring it, thereby planting the seed of suspicion that grows until both Eve and God "take the bait." Had Job ever been informed of this wager, it is easy to imagine that his anger against God for such cruel unbelief in him would have exceeded all his other desperate outbursts of rage against God.

Maybe the thrust of a sermon on this text should not be on explanations of suffering per se but on how we relate to God in the midst of great hardships and losses. With that focus in view, we have incomplete data in the resigned Job of the prologue. We must add into the balance not only his initial acceptance of his plight but also his subsequent titanic protest and argument with God, which itself comes to comprise a major part of his expression of faith. And we must also take account of his eventual "reunion" with God which has, as we shall see, an indeterminate quality. It may even be wondered in what sense Job can be a model for us, since he is presented as "one of a kind," unexcelled and unequaled in his piety, which is certainly not something any of us would dare to claim for ourselves. To preach on Job is a good antidote for dogmatism and self-assurance in the pulpit, and it might do congregations good to see a preacher admit to limitations of wisdom.

Movies: *A Little Princess* (1995); *The Wrong Man* (1958).

JOB 23:1-9, 16-17; WISDOM OF SOLOMON 7:7-11 (21st Sunday/Proper 23)

In the dialogues with his friends, Job shows his "true colors," so to speak. Breaking out of stoic resignation, he heatedly affirms his innocence of any sins meriting the magnitude of what has befallen him. Moreover, he brazenly accuses God of brutalizing him and he appeals—yea, demands— that God appear and deal justly with his situation. Yet, try as he will, Job cannot locate God. His insistence on a personal audience with God gives way to frustration and utter despair. At the moment he feels sheer terror before God and he longs to disappear into darkness (as his wife advised him from the start). It takes little effort to empathize with Job, to recognize in his great agony what many of us who believe in God have experienced at times in our lives. It is cathartic to hear someone express such feelings as eloquently as the author of Job does. It is probably true to say that for faith to put down deep roots, we must be able to express our anger with God as directly and intensely as we express our praise and thanksgiving. A sermon on this text might compare the iconic virtues of the stoic Job of the prologue with the protesting despairing mood of Job in the poetry, not so much as polar opposites but as competing and complementary ways of coping with adversity—which often coexist in the same sufferer.

An alternative reading is proposed from Wisdom of Solomon 7:7-11 in the Roman Catholic lectionary. It is a paean to the spirit of wisdom, which is to be preferred above wealth, health, and beauty because, unlike those other goods, wisdom never ceases. Still, the writer ends by claiming that he can "have his cake and eat it too," because in espousing wisdom all the other good things came to him. Is there not here a touch of that easygoing confusion of wisdom and virtue with success that the Accuser had in mind when he doubted the depth of Job's piety?

Movies: *Crimes and Misdemeanors* (1989); *Philadelphia* (1993).

JOB 38:1-7, 34-41 (22nd Sunday/Proper 24)

When God finally speaks to Job out of the whirlwind, we are eager to hear some straightforward definitive word that will settle the matters that Job and his friends have disputed without any agreement. In fact, Job gets nothing like a definitive answer to his claims. Many interpreters take it that God disdains and belittles Job in order to humiliate and browbeat him into submission. It is certainly clear that God does not answer Job in the terms demanded. Instead of talking about Job's situation, he presents Job a panorama of divine activity in the wonders of the created world. On the other hand, some interpreters see a great honor accorded Job by the fact that God does speak to him, and that this very opening of communication is deeply consoling to Job—even when he is scarcely able to sustain his part of the conversation. They believe it significant that, in spite of all Job's rantings against deity—which stop barely short of the cursing that the Accuser predicted—the deity has not abandoned him but has answered his deepest desire to have an audience with God, even though it will be quite otherwise than Job expected. Exactly what twist we should put on God's speeches to Job depends in good measure on the tone of voice in which God spoke, if only we could hear that voice as the author imagined Job to have heard it. A homily on this reading might explore situations in our lives when God refuses to speak to us on the terms we present, but confronts us with uninvited and unnerving words.

Movies: *Moby Dick* (1956); *The Seventh Seal* (1945).

JOB 42:1-6, 10-17 (23rd Sunday/Proper 25)

The close of the poetic section of the book is not an unambiguous closure. Job does come to terms with God. He turns over in his mind God's challenging reminder that his knowledge is limited and that God is as much the questioner of him as he is the questioner of God. Job declares his satisfaction by saying, "Formerly I had heard of you, . . . but now my eye sees you." He has a fuller knowing experience of God without having his suffering explained to him.

The final remark of Job is among the most contested verses in the Bible (v. 6). Does he really despise himself and repent of his brashness in questioning God, as most translations of the text presuppose? Or does an equally plausible translation of the verse show Job withdrawing his case and accepting his status as a mere human who will always be of the earth, willingly—even joyfully—embracing "dust and ashes"? In the one case, as a self-despising sinner, he takes back everything he has previously argued. In the other case, as one who sees God and still lives, he gladly accepts his finitude before God and finds peace, yet without retracting any of his previous protestations.

The latter reading seems more accordant both with the power of Job's previous arguments and the following justification of Job in the epilogue, when God says to the friends, "you have not spoken of me what is right, as my servant Job has" (v. 7). This can only be understood as God's approval of Job's argument over against his friends. Intriguingly, this explicit approbation of Job's case against God is not spoken to Job, but indirectly to the friends.

In another surprising twist, the book ends with the restoration of Job's fortunes, further confounding us with what superficially looks like confirmation of the belief that piety is rewarded with prosperity. Given the whole book, the placid ending does not feel like a sop to traditionalism. The epilogue seems simply to say that the righteous aren't always prosperous and happy, but sometimes they are, at least at some times in their lives. And it couldn't happen to a worthier one than Job. Lots of sermonic material here for plumbing the power of a faith so deep that it dares to confront and question—even accuse—God.

Movies: *Passion Fish* (1992); *The Seventh Veil* (1945).

IV. Apocalyptic Texts

We turn now to several apocalyptic texts that picture a catastrophic end time leading to the defeat of evil empires that have ruled over Israel and the early church, and issuing finally in the triumphant rule of God over humankind. Apocalyptic literature (from a word meaning "revelation, unveiling") is dramatically pictorial, rich in symbolism, constituting a genre that is very like science fiction and fantasy literature. It abounds in visions, dreams, and symbolism; in its oppositional stance toward prevailing politics, it sketches stereotypes and caricatures in the manner of satirical political cartoons. As written, the texts expected an imminent end of history. Since such an end has not eventuated, generations of literalizing interpreters have fruitlessly attempted to fix a timetable for its arrival. In reaction to these naive misreadings, a majority of Jews and Christians have tended to ignore apocalyptic writings altogether.

DANIEL 7:9-14 (Christ the King Sunday/Proper 29)

The Danielic vision of the defeat of the four beasts (representing Babylonia, Media, Persia, and the Hellenistic empires) and the coming of the reign of "one like a Son of Man [= the Truly Human One]" appears in a writing that comes from the time of the Maccabean wars against Seleucid Syria, 167–164 B.C.E. The dream vision of Daniel is interpreted by an angelic mediator who explains that God, described as the Ancient One (or the Source of Time), will give dominion over the earth to the Truly Human One who is said to personify "the holy ones of the Most High" (v. 18). These "holy ones" or "saints" have been interpreted either as angels or as the law-observing Jews who resisted the attempts of Hellenized Jews and their Seleucid backers to impose a hybrid form of Greek-Jewish worship on the Jerusalem community. It is most likely that the just rule of pious Jews is here described in veiled form.

The Son of Man/Truly Human One personification appears in the Synoptic Gospels on the lips of Jesus, where it is far from clear whether Jesus uses it of himself or of another yet to come. It is used in contexts that anticipate the suffering and death of Jesus and the coming of the kingdom of God in full power. It is not a title by which his contemporaries address Jesus, nor is it a favorite term of the Gospel writers, who prefer Son of God and Christ/Messiah, and it soon disappears from early Christian usage in this apocalyptic sense. Eventually the church resumed the "Son of Man" title, this time to refer to the human dimensions of Jesus, in contrast to "Son of God" to indicate his divinity.

The concept of the Son of Man is complex and elusive. In the prophet Ezekiel it meant simply "mere mortal." In later apocalyptic tradition, particularly the Book of Enoch, it attained a special coloration derived from the notion that Enoch, transported permanently to heaven while still alive (Gen. 5:24), becomes the Messiah/Son of Man who will return to earth as the agent of God's judgment and rule. Daniel appears to recast the notion by making it a personification for an entire group of sanctified Jews. While Enoch will descend to earth to rule, Daniel seems to envision the Son of Man (= sanctified Jews) as transported to the throne of God in heaven where they receive the commission to rule on earth. Spatial imagery of earth below/heaven above is used in apocalyptic literature to represent both lesser power vs. highest power and to represent evil and suffering vs. future righteousness and deliverance. We have noted in Hebrews a similar dualistic portraiture of heaven vs. earth that seems to have been influenced by a blend of Platonic and apocalyptic sources (see Introduction to Letter Pathway [pp. 26–28], and Heb. 7:23-28).

The Danielic vision expresses the power of God to overcome evil in the world and to establish a rule of righteousness in which those who have been true to God will govern as God's agents. As recounted in 1 and 2 Maccabees, the rule of the Maccabees/Hasmoneans in Judah, once they gained independence from the Seleucid Empire, was far from utopian.

Probably the writer of Daniel would have had little sympathy for their corrupt and bloody power politics. Later attempts to implement this sort of vision in theopolitical programs, such as Calvin's Geneva, Cromwell's Britain, Puritan New England, Mormon Utah—and one might add the United States as some sectors of the Religious Right would like to have it be governed—have been dubious projects. Nonetheless, the anticipation that God's reign of peace and justice will one day be more fully realized on earth is a foundational concept that motivates us in our efforts to live out the way of Jesus as a prophetic movement toward the redemption of history. A worthy sermonic reflection might focus on how to maintain the hope of the kingdom as empowerment for just action in the world, while renouncing fanaticism, intolerance, and hateful violence that only repeat the history we have long known.

Movies: *The King of Hearts* (1966); *Watership Down* (1978).

DANIEL 12:1-13 (26th Sunday/Proper 28)

The final vision of Daniel includes a lengthy "prophecy" about the end time, which is actually a veiled recital by a heavenly messenger of past and present relations between the Ptolemaic and Seleucid Hellenistic empires (chap. 11). This pseudoprophecy culminates in the anticipated death of Antiochus Epiphanes who had profaned the Jerusalem temple. In the present pericope, the heavenly messenger, who is probably the Gabriel of 8:16 and 9:21, describes the impact of the final cataclysm on faithful and apostate Jews (vv. 1-3), and the book closes with directions to Daniel to seal up his writing until the final days have arrived (vv. 4-13).

Angels play a large role in Daniel as interpreters of dreams and visions and as warriors in cosmic battles that form the counterpart of struggles on earth. In this case it is said that Michael "shall arise, the great prince who has charge of your [Daniel's] people" (12:1), the same Michael who is described earlier as a "chief prince" who, together with Gabriel, has fought with the princes of Persia and Greece [the Ptolemaic and Seleucid Hellenistic empires] (10:13, 20-21). The context implies that the foreign nations have heavenly beings (fallen angels?) who protect and fight for them, just as the Jews are defended by heavenly beings loyal to God. The decisive deliverance of faithful Jews will occur when Michael prevails over the prince(s) of their Hellenistic oppressors.

The mode of deliverance for the faithful Jews is tersely but vividly described with the first, and only, certain reference to resurrection of the dead in the Old Testament. This will not be a general resurrection; only "many" of the dead will arise, evidently the most righteous and most wicked among them. The text seems to have in mind the law-observing martyrs of the Maccabean war and their Jewish opponents. The resurrected faithful will enjoy "everlasting life," while the resurrected apostates will suffer "shame and everlasting contempt." No details are given about the nature of the resurrected community in which the faithful and apostates alike will perpetually coexist in what appears to be "heaven on earth" for the former and "hell on earth" for the latter. The resurrected faithful are described as "the wise who turn many to righteousness" in language reminiscent of the servant figure in Isaiah 53. This sketch of the status of the Jewish saints following their resurrection is another way of speaking about the dominion over the earth that is given to the Son of Man/the Truly Human One who personifies "the saints of the Most High" in Daniel 7.

Shortly after Daniel was written, part of the visions was fulfilled: the temple was restored and the Hellenistic yoke was lifted from Israel. However, the cosmic overthrow of evil and enthronement of unimpeded righteousness on earth did not transpire. The everlasting reign of the saints failed to materialize. Because of this "nonfulfillment," the book of Daniel remained an open book that successive groups of Jews and Christians reinterpreted to refer to the crises through which they struggled in anticipation of the final redemption of history (as in Mark 13).

Most Christians realize the folly of thinking that the book of Daniel refers cryptically to the precise unfolding events that will precede the end of history. On the other hand, the apocalyptic mode of thought as a pictorial form of "utopian" hope is a powerful resource for envisioning the struggle between good and evil tendencies that has as its goal the triumph of a redeemed humanity in the kingdom of God. The symbolism of the resurrection motif that develops ever more fully in later Judaism and Christianity speaks of "the unfinished agenda" of justice and righteousness in human history. Death is not the final word on any given life or on human life as a whole. Apocalyptic thought has as its living spiritual core the challenge to struggle for the embodiment of God's reign on earth no matter what the odds at any given moment.

The power and the promise of this hope is not an ethereal abstraction, however. It has vital meaning only to those whose lives are committed in the day-to-day struggle to embody the kingdom of God. Here is a homiletical theme that can reach out from Daniel to ponder the resurrection of Jesus, who resisted evil even to death and, in doing so, overcame death proleptically for all who struggle with him. The message also reaches out to us. As it has been succinctly put, "without insurrection there is no resurrection." What are the contemporary devaluations and distortions of human life that we commit ourselves to resist? What is so significant and critical about our struggles to make us desire and have confidence in a resurrection for ourselves or for humans at large? More bluntly, is what we are doing with our lives worthy of being resurrected?

Movies: *Cocoon* (1985); *Resurrection* (1980).

MARK 13:1-32 (26th Sunday/Proper 28)

Compared to full-fledged apocalypses like Daniel and Revelation, the recorded teachings of Jesus are very modest in their scope and detail concerning the end of history and the coming kingdom of God. Jesus exudes a fundamental future-oriented confidence that God's hopes and promises for human life are, as it were, "the wave of the future," and he summons his followers to join that movement by helping to make the justice and mercy of God manifest in their relations with others here and now. The greater part of Jesus' teaching is more akin to Old Testament prophecy and wisdom than it is to apocalyptic.

Mark 13 is the one apparent exception to the distance Jesus otherwise keeps from apocalyptic schemes of thought. This lengthy discourse on the end times is recognizable as a product of early Christians who are facing persecution and who conceive Jesus speaking to their situation in concepts and images of apocalyptic coinage. The discourse is "attached" to a probably historical incident in which Jesus predicts the destruction of the temple based on a belief that its leadership and cult have betrayed their commission by God. The disciples want to know when this will happen; they ask for "signs." Elsewhere in the Gospels, Jesus is loath to give signs, preferring to let people recognize the "signs" inherent in his words and deeds. In this instance, however, he details an amalgam of cosmic and social disasters constituting "the birth pangs" of the end time: wars, earthquakes, famines, eclipses, persecutions, trials, executions, and competing claims to religious authority rending the Christian community. The situation envisioned is that of early Christians who are expelled from synagogues and brought to trial before civil authorities for disturbing the peace or for treason, in the manner described throughout the Book of Acts. Growing harassment, ostracism, and persecution create fertile ground for "false prophets" who claim to speak for God and "false messiahs" who claim to be Jesus returned to earth in this moment of crisis.

Where and when did the circumstances of early Christians here described take place? The clearest clue is the reference to "the desolating sacrilege set up where it ought not to be" (v. 14), which alludes unmistakably to the desecration of the temple in Maccabean times (Dan. 11:31; 12:11) and is here reappropriated to apply to a later such desecration, which most interpreters believe to be the destruction of the temple by the Romans in 70 C.E. In the Jewish uprising against Rome, Jewish Christians seem to have been caught between nationalist partisans of the war, on the one hand, and Roman authorities and Gentile citizens, on the other hand, and in the process suffered the abuse that often falls on those who do not align themselves with either side in warfare. The cryptic instruction, "let the reader understand," may be a way of calling attention to the Danielic source of the term "desolating sacrilege," or, more likely, a way of alluding to the contemporary sacrilege without actually stating it ("you all know to what I refer!").

A homily on this discourse might usefully focus on what happens in a Christian community when competing voices claim to speak for Jesus. "Many will come in my name and say, 'I am he!' . . . if anyone says to you at that time, 'Look! Here is the Messiah!' or 'Look! There he is!'—do not believe it" (vv. 6, 21). Fanatics who claim to be Jesus have little appeal today, but there are many voices claiming to speak "in his name." Competing religious, social, and political programs and policies are widely claimed to be what Jesus would approve if he were alive today. Mesmerizing leaders in church and society speak with dogmatic authority, often trumpeting single issues and "snowing" their opponents with moralistic rhetoric. Their demagoguery exudes a "messianic" aura that solicits uncritical adulation from the public.

How are we to evaluate these seductive voices? How do we judge what is an authentic implementation of the spirit of Jesus? Among the time-tested criteria are these: Do the analyses and proposals of those claiming the mantle of Jesus's approval square with his teachings and with his life? Are they conducive to respect and concern for the needs and interests of all people affected by their ideas and plans? Do they ring true to the weight of Christian tradition and experience? What motives do they appeal to, and what is the depth of their understanding of the issues they propound? Religious and political discourse would be immeasurably improved if these yardsticks were applied to all would-be leaders in church and society.

Movies: *The Ruling Class* (1972); *Whistle Down the Wind* (1962).

REVELATION 1:1-8 (Christ the King Sunday/Proper 29)

The book of Revelation is a hybrid work composed of letters to seven church in Asia Minor and a series of apocalyptic visions of the ultimate triumph of the kingdom of God and of Jesus Christ. It is intended to strengthen the faithful endurance of its readers and to prompt them to good works in the midst of hostility and persecution from without and despair and apathy within. The crucified Jesus will become the victorious Christ, and Christians who have been persecuted or martyred will find solace in a transformed heaven and earth. The book draws heavily on Old Testament traditions, especially Daniel. In the opening verses alone we encounter "the kingdom of priests" from Exod. 19:6, "the one coming on the clouds" from Dan. 7:13, and "the one whom they have pierced" from Zech. 12:10.

Revelation alone among apocalyptic writings names its actual writer, a certain John who is imprisoned on Patmos for his Christian confession, and it also names the seven churches whose members are the addressees of the book. It is intended to be read aloud in those churches (v. 3), and it opens with a salutation typical of letters (v. 4). It probably was written during the persecutions unleashed by the Roman emperor Domitian in the last decade of the first century C.E.

Amidst the chilling details of its visions, it is replete with outbursts of praise and adoration of God and Christ, a worshipful tone struck already in the doxology of vv. 5b-6. It entertains a spacious view of God "who is and who was and who is to come" (vv. 4, 8), who declares, "I am the Alpha and the Omega, and the beginning and the end" (v. 8). Jesus Christ is the "faithful witness," whose "testimony" concerning God is in turn "testified to" by God's servant John (vv. 1, 2). The christological crux of Revelation is that the crucified and resurrected Christ is to be manifest as "the ruler of the kings of the earth" (v. 5) whose rule will give way to God's rule through Christ.

Revelation is resistant to easy reading, not alone because of its fanciful imagery, but chiefly because it presupposes extreme crisis in Christian communities facing a hostile, death-dealing environment. That is not the felt experience of most of our mainline churches in the United States, although it is a keenly felt experience in many Third World churches and it resonates in those churches in our land that are in touch with the pain and suffering of marginalized people in our society. Even when dutifully studied, Revelation will remain a puzzling document to those who have not experienced the suffering of Christ in their own sufferings or in the sufferings of those around them—whether near at hand or farther away.

A sermon on this pericope might explore what it means to envision Christ as "the ruler of the kings of the earth," when most of our current theology views him mainly as the lord of our personal lives. What is the world historical meaning of this claim? What are the theological conceptual grounds that allow John to spin out such a fearful and wondrous cosmic fantasy? Does the affirmed ultimate rule of Christ over all human institutions mean that they are rejected as of no value, or does his rule mean that what is of value and merit in those institutions is incorporated and perfected in his rule? What are the practical implications of this kind of faith for us in our daily lives and for the outlook and activities of our churches? How do we narrow the gap between our devotion to Christ as savior of souls and our commitment to Christ as the judge and savior of our common human life?

Movies: *Pale Rider* (1985); *The Seventh Sign* (1948).

LECTIONARY CHARTS

Twentieth Sunday after Pentecost
Twenty-Seventh Sunday in Ordinary Time / Proper 22

Lectionary	First Lesson	Psalm	Second Lesson	Gospel
Revised Common	Job 1:1; 2:1-10 or Gen. 2:18-24	Psalm 26 or 8	Heb. 1:1-4; 2:5-12	Mark 10:2-16
Episcopal (BCP)	Gen. 2:18-24	Psalm 8 or 128	Heb. 2:(1-8) 9-18	Mark 10:2-9
Roman Catholic	Gen. 2:18-24	Ps. 128:1-6	Heb. 2: 9-11	Mark 10:2-16 or Mark 10:2-12
Lutheran (LBW)	Gen. 2:18-24	Psalm 128	Heb. 2: 9-11 (12-18)	Mark 10:2-16

Twenty-First Sunday after Pentecost
Twenty-Eighth Sunday in Ordinary Time / Proper 23

Lectionary	First Lesson	Psalm	Second Lesson	Gospel
Revised Common	Job 23:1-9, 16-17 or Amos 5:6-7, 10-15	Ps. 22:1-15 or Ps. 90:12-17	Heb. 4:12-16	Mark 10:17-31
Episcopal (BCP)	Amos 5:6-7, 10-15	Psalm 90 or Ps. 90:1-8, 12	Heb. 3:1-6	Mark 10:17-27 (28-31)
Roman Catholic	Wisd. 7:7-11	Ps. 90:12-17	Heb. 4:12-13	Mark 10:17-30 or Mark 10:17-27
Lutheran (LBW)	Amos 5:6-7, 10-15	Ps. 90:12-17	Heb. 3:1-6	Mark 10:17-27 (28-30)

Twenty-Second Sunday after Pentecost
Twenty-Ninth Sunday in Ordinary Time / Proper 24

Lectionary	First Lesson	Psalm	Second Lesson	Gospel
Revised Common	Job 38:1-7, (34-41) or Isa. 53:4-12	Ps. 104:1-9, 24, 35c or Ps. 91:9-16	Heb. 5:1-10	Mark 10:35-45
Episcopal (BCP)	Isa. 53:4-12	Psalm 91 or Ps. 91:9-16	Heb. 4:12-16	Mark 10:35-45
Roman Catholic	Isa. 53:10-11	Ps. 33:4-5, 18-19, 20, 22	Heb. 4:14-16	Mark 10:35-45 or Mark 10: 42-45
Lutheran (LBW)	Isa. 53:10-12	Ps. 91:9-16	Heb. 4:9-16	Mark 10:35-45

Twenty-Third Sunday after Pentecost
Thirtieth Sunday in Ordinary Time / Proper 25

Lectionary	First Lesson	Psalm	Second Lesson	Gospel
Revised Common	Job 42:1-6, 10-17 or Jer. 31:7-9	Ps. 34:1-8 (19-22) or Psalm 126	Heb. 7:23-28	Mark 10:46-52
Episcopal (BCP)	Isa. 59:(1-4) 9-19	Psalm 13	Heb. 5:12—6:1, 9-12	Mark 10:46-52
Roman Catholic	Jer. 31:7-9	Ps. 126:1-6	Heb. 5:1-6	Mark 10:46-52
Lutheran (LBW)	Jer. 31:7-9	Psalm 126	Heb. 5:1-10	Mark 10:46-52

Twenty-Fourth Sunday after Pentecost
Thirty-First Sunday in Ordinary Time / Proper 26

Lectionary	First Lesson	Psalm	Second Lesson	Gospel
Revised Common	Ruth 1:1-18 or Deut. 6:1-9	Psalm 146 or Ps. 119:1-8	Heb. 9:11-14	Mark 12:28-34
Episcopal (BCP)	Deut. 6:1-9	Ps. 119:1-16 or Ps. 119:1-8	Heb. 7:23-28	Mark 12:28-34
Roman Catholic	Deut. 6:2-6	Ps. 18:2-4, 47, 51	Heb. 7:23-28	Mark 12:28-34
Lutheran (LBW)	Deut. 6:1-9	Ps. 119:1-16	Heb. 7:23-28	Mark 12:28-34 (35-37)

Twenty-Fifth Sunday after Pentecost
Thirty-Second Sunday in Ordinary Time / Proper 27

Lectionary	First Lesson	Psalm	Second Lesson	Gospel
Revised Common	Ruth 3:1-5; 4:13-17 or 1 Kings 17:8-16	Psalm 127 or Psalm 146	Heb. 9:24-28	Mark 12:38-44
Episcopal (BCP)	1 Kings 17:8-16	Psalm 146 or Ps. 146:4-9	Heb. 9:24-28	Mark 12:38-44
Roman Catholic	1 Kings 17:10-16	Ps. 146:2, 7-10	Heb. 9:24-28	Mark 12:38-44 or Mark 12:41-44
Lutheran (LBW)	1 Kings 17:8-16	Ps. 107:1-3, 33-43	Heb. 9:24-28	Mark 12:41-44

Twenty-Sixth Sunday after Pentecost
Thirty-Third Sunday in Ordinary Time / Proper 28

Lectionary	First Lesson	Psalm	Second Lesson	Gospel
Revised Common	I Sam. 1:4-20 or Dan. 12:1-3	I Sam. 2:1-10 or Psalm 16	Heb. 10:11-14, (15-18), 19-25	Mark 13:1-8
Episcopal (BCP)	Dan. 12:1-4a (5-13)	Psalm 16 or Ps. 16:5-11	Heb. 10:31-39	Mark 13:14-23
Roman Catholic	Dan. 12:1-3	Ps. 16:1, 5, 8-11	Heb. 10: 11-14, 18	Mark 13:24-32
Lutheran (LBW)	Dan. 12:1-3	Psalm 16	Heb. 10: 11-18	Mark 13:1-13

Christ the King
Last Sunday after Pentecost
Thirty-Fourth Sunday in Ordinary Time / Proper 29

Lectionary	First Lesson	Psalm	Second Lesson	Gospel
Revised Common	2 Sam. 23:1-7 or Dan. 7:9-10, 13-14	Ps. 132:1-12, (13-18) or Psalm 93	Rev. 1:4b-8	John 18:33-37
Episcopal (BCP)	Dan. 7:9-14	Psalm 93	Rev. 1:1-8	John 18:33-37 or Mark 11:1-11
Roman Catholic	Dan. 7:13-14	Ps. 93:1-2, 5	Rev. 1:5-8	John 18:33-37
Lutheran (LBW)	Dan. 7:13-14	Psalm 93	Rev. 1:4b-8	John 18:33-37